ISBN: 978-0-9935157-3-6

www.celinenaughton.com

Contents

Where better to start a series about the Easter Rising than in the very building where the rebels of 1916 made their headquarters - the GPO in Dublin's O'Connell Street? I hoped that An Post Director of Communications Barney Whelan would talk me through the plans for the ambitious 'Witness History' exhibition, then in mid-construction. Instead, he invited me on a personal tour of the historic site, so I donned the hard hat and boots and got a private preview of one of Dublin's most iconic visitor attractions as it was being built. I saw massive columns being erected, wandered past the area where a giant curved video screen would bring people as close to the action as you could imagine, then upstairs through what would become an art gallery and café, and finally out on to the courtyard where, very clearly, I got my first glimpse of the ghosts of 1916.

A Walk Through History
with the Ghosts of the GPO

It's a bright morning in early August 2015, sunlight is streaming through the windows, outside the traffic rumbles its daily course along O'Connell Street and here inside the General Post Office, An Post Communications Director Barney Whelan leads me on an exclusive tour of Irish history's most iconic building.

On a day like this it's hard to visualise the harsh reality of 1916 when artillery shells blasted off the walls and bullets bounced off the concrete, but plans are afoot to retell the famous story in a way it's never been told before.

No newspaper has yet stepped foot on to the site of the multi-million redevelopment of the GPO that's widely regarded as one of the most important projects of the 2016 commemorations, but the *Irish Independent* has managed to get a sneak peek.

We stand for a moment on the balcony overlooking the main post office, a bustling centre that sees 120,000 people come through its doors every year. Is it possible James Connolly or Patrick Pearse might have stood in this very spot leading the rebels within?

"Not here – just down there," points Barney to an area below where people are quietly going about their business across a polished floor. "That's where they most likely set up their base."

How utterly different the scene must have been with rebel soldiers holding out against attack and Cumann na mBan women tending to the wounded. Their ghosts are everywhere in this building and soon their voices will be heard again when the GPO opens its doors to bring one of the most pivotal times in Irish history to life.

"My 1916 started in 2011," says Barney, explaining that's when the team at An Post started to float ideas for the centenary commemorations.

"Put on a play," said one.

"Have an exhibition," said another.

Barney wanted more. It's not just another historic building, after all. This was the heart of the action, the rebel HQ, the place where Pearse read the Proclamation asserting Ireland's right to freedom. He had to think big.

"Yes, create an exhibition, but make it a permanent one,

not just some candyfloss that would be over and done with by the end of 2016," he says. "This is an opportunity for people to really engage with the building and our history. We had to produce a lasting legacy for the nation."

And what a legacy it promises to be: there's an exhibition centre bringing events of one hundred years ago into the 21st Century, an art gallery, café, shop and an open courtyard that can be used for different things, not least as a place to reflect. His plans were warmly received at an all-party committee in 2012, but the question was, where would the money come from?

"Securing funding was the most challenging part of the entire process. I knew we had something special, but An Post couldn't afford it and money was tight. It was an enormous relief when Jimmy Deenihan (then Minister for Arts, Heritage and Gaeltacht Affairs) gave it the green light."

In Autumn 2013, the figure was approved in the Budget and from then on, it was full steam ahead.

"Suddenly, we went from all talk to all work. It was like a horse bolting and we've been charging forward ever since towards that no-pressure deadline of March 25th 2016. We started by giving the building a good clean, something that hadn't happened since its completion in 1929. There was never enough money, but now we set to cleaning, restoring and conserving the facades."

He shows me a scale model of the planned redevelopment before we gear up in hard hats and high-vis vests to walk through the real thing. Downstairs, work is in full swing to create the exhibition space. Concrete columns are being polished and specialist lighting and air systems intalled in a vast room dominated by a semi-circular feature where gigantic screens will show videos and images while groups hear talks about the Rising. Beyond it is a children's educational area laid out like a 1916 barricade, where kids will face such challenges as how to reconnect broken communication lines.

Elsewhere, booths with touch-screen technology will provide information in a way that caters for all ages "from schoolchildren to scholars." Over 300,000 visitors a year are expected to flood this space.

"The permanent exhibition will put the Easter Rising into a social, political and cultural context," says Barney. "It will deal with events leading up to the Rising, the Rising itself, the proclamation, the aftermath and the consequences."

We climb the stairs to what will be a gallery depicting how 1916 was commemorated over the following one hundred years. With a café and shop at one end, the gallery opens out on to a bright, open courtyard, where a monument will honour the forty children killed during the Rising.

"Joe Duffy has uncovered harrowing tales," says Barney. "Some babies died in their mother's arms from bullets that went through their mothers. Others were young boys, teenagers shot while looting."

Already it's the kind of space that beckons you to linger, but it's time to leave. Among the hordes outside on the busy street is a group of evangelists handing out leaflets with the headline: '*Is there life after death?*'

Who knows? But when it comes to the historic walls of the GPO, to borrow from W.B. Yeats, "*We can write but one line that is certain, 'Here are ghosts.'*"

I couldn't wait to talk to Irish author Orna Ross about her novels 'After the Rising' and 'Before the Fall,' because I absolutely fell in love with them - truly, madly, deeply. Now, I happen to know Orna - we worked together back in the '80s, before she became a global publishing phenomenon - and I know what you're thinking; how can I possibly be objective about the work of somebody I've declared is a personal acquaintance? All I can say is trust me, read her books for yourself. This is superb storytelling, end of. As the novels are based in the era of the Easter Rising, the War of Independence and the Civil War, Orna was an obvious choice as a subject for 'My 1916.' And if you're as passionate as she is about the work of WB Yeats and his obsession with Maud Gonne, you'll no doubt also enjoy her latest work, 'Her Secret Rose.'

A Sense of Shame,
Cloaked in Silence

When Jo Devereux discovers her granny was once an Irish freedom fighter who hid arms under her coat, she sees the tiny, frail old woman she grew up with in a whole new light. It's one of a host of family secrets that come spilling out on the pages of *After the Rising*, Orna Ross's bestselling novel that brings events of the 1916 Rising and subsequent Civil War to life in a way that history books often can't.

The story, and its sequel, *Before the Fall*, deal with the effects of that pivotal era in Irish history on relationships between families, friends and entire communities that continue right up to this very day.

The inspiration came from Orna's own family history and upbringing in a small Co. Wexford village. Ireland at that time was full of such villages where, she says, "some families drank in one pub and others in another and never the twain would meet. Whole generations didn't speak to each other.

"Even as children, we knew which kids we should and shouldn't hang out with, and nobody told us why. We were just born to it."

For a child growing up in the 1960s and '70s, the community's self-imposed segregation was bewildering, and explanations were neither proffered nor sought.

"That generation was kept in place by silence," she says. "There were things you just didn't talk about – like anything to do with sexual politics, women's reproductive rights, unmarried pregnancy, domestic violence…"

And the war. Especially don't mention the war.

"For me, the Easter Rising and the Civil War are interconnected. You can't talk about one without the other. But while the Rising was portrayed as a glorious event, people were ashamed by what followed six years later."

Dublin may have dominated the action during Easter week 1916, but it wasn't the only place to rise against British rule. Just eighty miles south of the capital, Wexford rebels concentrated their efforts in Enniscorthy, where they seized the town for five days and blocked the roads and railway line to prevent troops getting through to Dublin.

"My grand aunt – whose proud boast was that De Valera once stayed in our house while visiting Wexford in 1932 – had been in Cumann na mBan and during the Civil War she was on the side of the 'Irregulars,' as those against the Treaty were known. It was only after her death I discovered her brother had been shot by his best friend during the Civil War. That shocked me! How could two men who'd been close friends growing up and comrades in the War of Independence become sworn enemies?"

She turned to her father, but he had no answers.

"The older generation had told him nothing. There was a sense of shame, cloaked in silence.

"My father inherited the mantle of Fianna Fail, until the Haughey era, when he became disillusioned and gave up on the party. From my perspective, I could never see a difference between either side. It was a divide that shouldn't be, a waste of political energy.

"I rejected it all, but when you reject something, you're not indifferent, so later I had to explore what it was I was turning my back on. I always knew I'd write about it. Even at the age of fourteen, I told a friend that one day I'd write a book about that time in history and how it affected us all.

"I saw at first hand how divisive the legacy of that era had become and how it filtered down through generations. The Rising was theatre, it changed hearts and minds, while the Civil War was an absolute tragedy.

"To quote W.B. Yeats, one of my heroes, '*great hatred, little room, maimed us at the start*'."

After The Rising became an international bestseller and launched Orna's career as an author and poet. She went on to found the Alliance of Independent Authors and is now rated by *The Bookseller* magazine as one of the top 100 most influential people in publishing in the world.

"I was part of the fight for women's rights in Ireland in the 1980s. It's the same drive towards autonomy that fires my work for indie authors," she says. "And, indeed, it was a drive for autonomy that created the Easter Rising in 1916.

"People have a right to express themselves and to my mind, self-expression is a right for all, not a privilege for the few. The stigma that exists around writers who self-publish doesn't sit well with me."

In August 2015 she launched the crowd-funded publication of *Secret Rose*, a special commemorative double-book containing Orna's novel, *Her Secret Rose*, about the turbulent relationship between W.B. Yeats and Maud Gonne, and *The Secret Rose*, his talismanic short stories.

"His publisher back then mutilated *The Secret Rose*," says Orna. "Yeats had meticulously laid out the sequence of stories in the order he wanted them, and the publisher Arthur Henry Bullen removed the final two, which eviscerated the whole meaning of his book."

A member of the Irish Republican Brotherhood in his earlier years, Yeats had distanced himself from nationalist politics by the time of the Rising, and only released his powerful poem *Easter, 1916*, four years after the event.

"Yeats and Lady Gregory became part of a cultural revolution as opposed to a political one," says Orna. "To mark the 150th anniversary of his birth, I wanted to pay tribute by putting his stories back together as he originally intended them to be read in 1897, alongside my own novel, all bound in a cover replicating his first edition."

Her Secret Rose, After the Rising and *Before the Fall* by Orna Ross are available on Amazon, iBooks and Kobo.

My dear friend Fergus D'Arcy, Emeritus Professor of modern history at UCD, steered me in the direction of the Royal Irish Academy, where Managing Editor Ruth Hegarty was overseeing the production of a number of specially commissioned books to commemorate the Easter Rising. Books published by the RIA are objects of beauty, painstakingly researched by experts in their field, illustrated by renowned artists, and printed and bound to exacting standards. (One of them, '1916: Portraits and Lives' features a biography of James Connolly written by none other than one Fergus D'Arcy). When I called, Ruth was insanely busy with print deadlines, launches, events and meetings all over the country. How on earth would she find time to talk to me? No problem, she said, I'd love to. How about Monday? As they say, ask a busy person...

The Woman with
the Golden Gun

Long before the Russians had women snipers fighting for the Red Army during World War Two, Ireland had her own femme fatale picking off the enemy during the Easter Rising.

One of the lesser known figures of 1916, Margaret Skinnider would regularly don her dark green Irish Citizen Army uniform to take pot shots from the Royal College of Surgeons. Then she'd put on a dress and cycle into the city to pass on a message, after which she'd return, pull on her soldier's breeches and start shooting again. And if that doesn't already sound like a character who'd give James Bond a run for his Moneypenny, she was also given to smuggling detonators concealed in her hat, then testing them with Countess Markievicz in the Dublin mountains.

Hers is one of forty-two biographies detailed in *1916: Portraits and Lives*, being published by the Royal Irish Academy (RIA). While Pearse, Clarke and key British figures feature large, it also gives the perspectives of less prominent characters, and Skinnider is one of Managing Editor Ruth Hegarty's favourites.

"She was fearless and fascinating in equal measure," she says. "When Mallin rejected her plan to hurl a bomb from a passing bicycle into the British-occupied Shelbourne Hotel as too risky for a woman, she argued that, as women were equal with men under the Irish Republic, they had an equal right to risk their lives."

Two years ago the RIA started planning for the 1916 commemorations and, as with the best-laid plans, the project snowballed as it rolled closer to the date. One book became two, then three… and the first hit a snag.

RIA books are typically big, quality tomes, but the photos for *Portraits and Lives* had not weathered well over the past hundred years. The ideal solution would be to commission original portraits, but it was an expensive option.

"We talked with the Office of Public Works, who commissioned them for the State Collection," says Ruth. "They will be exhibited at Kilmainham Gaol and we will use the portraits for the book.

The portraits steered her on to a new train of thought: fifteen railway stations throughout the country are named after rebel leaders of 1916, so she got in touch with Irish Rail.

"Some people may not realise that Pearse Station is named after both brothers, Patrick and Willie, or that Kingsbridge became known as Heuston Station in honour of Sean Heuston; at twenty-five, one of the younger rebel leaders to be executed.

"Casement Station in Tralee is named after Roger Casement, arrested when he landed on Banna Strand on Good Friday 1916 and later hanged and buried at Pentonville Prison in London: forty-nine years later he was granted a State funeral and reinterred in Glasnevin.

"Plunkett Station in Waterford commemorates Joseph Mary Plunkett, who married Grace Gifford in Kilmainham Gaol the day before his execution."

Irish Rail embraced the idea and agreed to display a gigantic poster of the relevant figure by artist David Rooney at these stations. A QR code is included in each display panel so that commuters can also download the chapter of the book about that person to find out more about the man after which each station is named.

"If 1916 encouraged a sense of working together, the people involved would surely have been impressed at the collaborative effort running through the centenary preparations," says Ruth. "There's something deeply satisfying about that."

She's also collaborating with historian Lucy McDiarmid on another book, *At Home in the Revolution*, which looks at the role women played during the Rising.

"It's full of eye-witness accounts from women who cooked

for the men, treated their wounds, and in some cases had their hearts broken by having to say their final farewells to their loved ones before they were executed... women like Eily O'Hanrahan and her sister who spent precious minutes with their brother Mícheál in Kilmainham Gaol the night before he was shot.

'*We said goodbye to Mícheál,*' Eily wrote. '*He did not weep, but kept up his courage. We did not give way either then. He kissed us several times and told us to give his love to Mother and Máire and to Harry when we found out where he was… We came downstairs and I got weak, and when I got to the ground floor I fainted.*'

"Discovering these stories – in the words of the people themselves – puts you in the picture as to what it must have been like to have lived during 1916," says Ruth. "I'm not a historian, but working with our authors has opened up a whole new world for me.

"I see places on my way to work that I never noticed before, like Connaught Street in Phibsboro, where Bulmer Hobson, an opponent of the Rising, was held at gunpoint in Michael Conlan's house, a few doors down from the O'Hanrahans, to prevent him trying to quash the insurrection.

"His fiancée Claire Gregan turned up at the door looking for him, but was told he wasn't there.

"Claire later wrote: '*Bulmer told me afterwards he heard me and made a move to come to the door and that another Volunteer guarding him pointed a gun at him.*'

"It's these kind of stories that bring the Easter Rising to life for me and I hope they will do so for generations to come."

Stephen Dunford is an author, historian and musician who also organises and takes part in grand scale historical re-enactments. He also has a gift for storytelling, as I discovered when he transported me to another era where I could hear the tramp of marching feet as 2,000 Franco-Irish fighters converged on Castlebar... What? This wasn't 1916! He'd taken me further back, to 1798 and the Year of the French. "What's that got to do with the Easter Rising?" I asked. "Everything," Stephen insisted, as he proceeded to explain how the leaders of 1916 had been inspired by Wolfe Tone and his fellow rebels from over a hundred years earlier. Not only did Stephen give me a new perspective, over the following months he would be so generous with his time, knowledge and contacts that I ended up calling him NT, short for National Treasure.

'The Rising's Foundations Were Laid
One Hundred Years Earlier'

It was that rarest of events in Irish history: a 2,000-strong force of Irish rebels and their French allies routed a much larger force of British regulars and militia in a famous victory known in revolutionary lore as "The Races of Castlebar," because of the speed with which the defeated Crown forces reputedly ran away.

This was the high point of the 1798 rebellion, which led to the foundation of the short-lived 'Republic of Connaught' and for a brief moment Ireland embraced the ideals of the French Revolution – 'Liberty, Equality and Fraternity.'

It's a stirring tale, but at a time when everyone is looking back to the Rising of 1916 rather than the rebellion of 1798, it hardly seems relevant. Mayo historian Stephen Dunford emphatically disagrees. According to him, without 1798 there could never have been a 1916. And so passionate is he on the point that he is, quite literally, prepared to pick up a pike or shoulder a musket to prove it.

Because in 2016, while so many eyes will be focused on commemorations in Dublin, Mayo will reverberate to the sounds, smells and smoke of battle as Stephen leads his troops in a series of re-enactments pertaining to 1798 and 'the Year of the French.'

"The 1916 Rising was a game-changer, but its foundations were laid over a hundred years earlier," says Stephen, the man behind 'In Humbert's Footsteps,' which scooped the 'National Gathering Event of the Year' award in 2013, and plans are afoot to ensure the centenary events are more spectacular than ever.

It was in Kilcummin, north of Killala, where General Jean Joseph Amable Humbert landed in August 1798. With Killala and Ballina garrisoned, and with Irish Volunteers flocking to the ranks, albeit not in the vast numbers promised by the United Irish leaders in France, Humbert's new Franco-Irish army departed Ballina, marching by night through the mountains to Castlebar, where upwards of 3,500 British soldiers awaited them.

With only one cannon and a combined Franco-Irish force of just 2,000, many armed only with pikes and pitchforks, Humbert succeeded in defeating the British commanded by the infamous General Lake.

But what have these events that took place over a century

earlier got to do with the Easter Rising?

"The principles of Republicanism that the French brought to Ireland – liberty, equality and fraternity – left a lasting legacy. When Ireland rose again in 1916, Pearse, Clarke and the other leaders of that rebellion looked to the likes of Wolfe Tone, John Moore and Bartholemew Teeling for inspiration.

"Teeling, a Lisburn man, was renowned for his bravery, valour and humanity, and became General Humbert's chief aide de camp. He, Wolfe Tone and the other leaders aspired to rule the country without bigotry or religious divide. This was the kind of republic they wanted for Ireland, and it's what the 1916 rebels fought for too."

Stephen's re-enactors too come from all walks of life, at home and abroad: at the 2013 re-enactment a bugler from the Orange Order played *The Last Post* in Castlebar.

"There's a huge cross-border, cross-community sharing of resources in our work and I'm heartened by the young people we meet," he says. "They don't see labels, they see a person.

"Recently, a young woman in her twenties told me her first memory of the Troubles in the North was of the Good Friday Agreement. I found that very gratifying, and so full of hope; it was a sign that out of all the conflicts in our history, we're finally moving on."

He believes that playing out historical events also brings history to life, whether it's the "mighty sight" of the Tall Ships he hopes will sail through Kilcummin next year, or the spectacle of hundreds of uniformed volunteers setting up camp in the old military barracks in Ballina before marching to battle.

"Last year we had 20,000 spectators on the streets of Ballina for one battle and we anticipate even bigger crowds right across the county for the centenary. People really get into the spirit of the re-enactment, and children love it. Last year, a kid from Breaffy National School said to me, 'Thanks a million for the best weekend of my life!' That was pretty rewarding, I can tell you."

What Stephen promises will be "the biggest event west of the Shannon" will take place in August. For Easter 2016, however, he'll be heading east to take part in re-enactments in Wexford and Kildare.

He has a personal connection with the Rising, as his paternal grandfather took part in the rebellion, but like many of his peers, the memories of that time went with him to the grave. However, his silence didn't dampen his grandson's passion for history.

"Every time I pass the 'Flagstone of the Green Moss' at Kilcummin, the spot where Humbert and the first contingent of French army came ashore, I am moved. History really resonates with me, and from my point of view, both 1798 and 1916 are inextricably linked," says Stephen.

"W.B. Yeats and Lady Gregory set their play *Kathleen Ní Houlihan* to the backdrop of the 1798 rebellion in Mayo and Killala in particular. And the revolutionary Maud Gonne, widow of John MacBride, unveiled a monument to General Humbert in Ballina in 1898.

"The connections between both rebellions are strong, and it's important they're kept alive because, managed properly, this country has a great future in its past."

Close to where General Humbert landed at Kilcummin, Co. Mayo in 1798 is the village of Foghill, birthplace of Micheál MacRuaidhrí. Described by Eoin MacNeill as "the greatest seanchaí of our time," MacRuaidhrí was a gardener and close confidant of Padraig Pearse. He was also a leading figure in the Gaelic revival and the author of five books in the Irish language. However, being illiterate, he relied on his only child Brighid to transcribe his stories, which she did dutifully at the kitchen table of their home in the gate lodge at St Enda's, Pearse's school in Rathfarnham. Brighid's daughter Phil Lynch told me how she herself sat in the same room as a child, being home-schooled by Pearse's sister Margaret. With such a glimpse into one family's life over just two generations, the people and events of 1916 feel not so distant at all.

Raised on Songs and Stories
of the Rising

Pádraig Pearse may have employed him as a gardener at St
Enda's school in the decade leading up the Rising, but there
was a lot more to Micheál Mac Ruaidhrí than tending flowers
and shrubs.

At a time when Pearse's own father had died, Mayo-born
Mac Ruaidhrí became like a father figure to the renowned rebel
leader of 1916.

Born with poor eyesight, Micheál Mac Ruaidhrí spent little
time at school and as an adult he couldn't read or write, but
notwithstanding this he went on to become one of the best
known figures of the Gaelic revival in the closing years of the
19th Century.

He began as a child, going from house to house, listening

to stories. As an adult, he was dubbed "the greatest seanchaí of our time" by Eoin MacNeill.

His friendship with Pearse began after he went to Dublin, where he worked as a gardener for the well-do-do and gave Irish language classes. Not only did Padraig Pearse give him a job tending the school gardens in Rathfarnham, he provided a house for Micheál and his wife Alice in the gate lodge after their marriage in 1911. The couple had one child, Brighid, born the following year.

"My mother was the only girl in St Enda's," says her daughter Phil Lynch, who grew up in the gate lodge and now lives in her own family home in a very different Rathfarnham from the country village of her childhood.

"From the age of ten, Brighid used to sit at the table dutifully writing down her father's stories, looking up now and then to gaze out the window, wishing she could be allowed to play outside."

But it wasn't only legend and lore that Micheál strove to protect; he also had great aspirations for an Irish Republic and during Easter week, he made his way to the GPO to fight for his country and stand next to his boss, then thirty-six years to Micheál's fifty-four.

"He spent a day there, but Pearse sent him home to look after his mother and sister, and his own wife and child," says Phil. "He told Micheál, 'Look after the women.'

"Pearse mentioned my grandfather in a song he wrote for his mother before he died:

'*Slán leat a Micheál ,*
Slán leat go deo,
Slán leat a Micheál ,
As Contae Mhuigheo. '"

After the Rising, Micheál was arrested with other rebels and detained in Frongoch prison in Wales, where he recited the rosary for his fellow inmates and taught them Irish. On his release, he took up his work and residence again at St Enda's until he died. The gate lodge remained Brighid's family home when she married in 1946 and it's where she raised her four children; a fifth died as a baby.

"Margaret Pearse, Padraig's sister, hosted my parents' wedding breakfast," says Phil. "There was a photo in the *Irish Press* about it. There was no alcohol, because Margaret was a pioneer. My grandfather's friend FX Coghlan gave her away. He was leader of the Rathfarnham branch of the Republican Army and often carried a gun. Once, when he was up at the gate lodge, there was a raid on the house. He jumped out the window and threw his gun in the hedge. Years later when the park was to be cleared, my mother told the authorities where to look for a gun and they found it in that very spot."

Phil was born the following year and Margaret Pearse was her godmother.

"Every year she gave me birthday presents and I'd go up to the big house to thank her. I didn't start school until the age of six, because Margaret insisted on home-schooling me until then. She sat at our kitchen table and taught me the alphabet."

Rathfarnham today is a bustling south Dublin suburb with an array of shops, schools, businesses and leisure amenities, but it was a very different place when Phil was a child.

"It wasn't built up like it is now. We were surrounded by fields. We didn't have electricity or running water and it never bothered us. We used candles and oil lamps, we washed in rainwater and got fresh water to drink from the big house. When electricity was finally installed, my mother was none too happy, because for the first time she could see all the dust in the house.

"My brother Tommy and I inherited our grandfather's love of gardening, but I'm afraid I'm not an Irish speaker. My mother was sorry she hadn't tried harder to make us all gaeilgeoirs – and she did try, believe me! – but the way Irish was taught when we were growing up was not very encouraging."

Micheál Mac Ruaidhrí died at home in 1936, at the age of seventy-six. On hearing the news, the then Taoiseach Eamon de Valera requested the coffin remain open until he paid his respects and when he got there, he formally saluted him.

"When my mother died in 2004, at the age of ninety-three, we laid her out here in my sitting room," says Phil. "I found it very moving when a friend of my son's, a young man in his twenties who used to sit enthralled listening to her stories growing up, came to pay his respects. After sitting with her for some time he strode over to her coffin and saluted her, just as Dev had done for my grandfather.

"We should be proud of the people who were part of the

Rising in 1916. I certainly am proud of my grandfather – and not only that he was part of the Easter Rising, but for his personal achievements too. He may have been uneducated, but he left behind a wealth of literature, folklore, poetry and stories. That's a legacy not just for our family but for the whole nation to treasure."

A soft-spoken civil servant and a most wanted man... Just who was this FX Coghlan Phil Lynch had mentioned, the daredevil who jumped out of a window and threw his gun into a hedge during a raid on her grandparents' house? She put me in touch with his grandson Gareth, who told me how Francis Xavier Coghlan had eluded the RIC so often, he was something of a Scarlet Pimpernel. They sought him here, they sought him there... and for years he hid in plain sight, just an ordinary man going about his business in the usual manner. But during the War of Independence, when his house was repeatedly raided by the Black and Tans and auxiliaries, he hid in a most unlikely place, often mere feet from the very men who were trying to hunt him down. As I was coming to realise, the 'ordinary' men and women of 1916 often did the most extraordinary things...

My Grandfather: A Forgotten Hero of 1916

FX Coghlan may be a forgotten hero of the Easter Rising, but painstaking research by his grandson reveals an intrepid fighter and master organiser who topped the British authorities' 'Most Wanted' list in the years following 1916.

On the surface, there was nothing to suspect the soft-spoken Cork man of being anything more than your average civil servant. He worked as a clerk in the Land Commission, played handball, went to mass and lived quietly with his wife and children in Dublin.

However, underneath the veneer of mediocrity, Francis Xavier Coghlan became such a force within the Republican movement that the Royal Irish Constabulary spared no effort to hunt him down, only to be outwitted every time.

"They raided the house so often, he dug a tunnel under the bath, about the size of a coffin, and would climb in there while the Black and Tans and auxiliaries combed the place," says his grandson Gareth Coghlan, who now shares the family home in Rathfarnham with his mother Éilís, seventy-nine, and uncle Dermot, seventy-eight.

"Once they camped out in the garden waiting for him to appear, and it's said he stayed for nine days in that hiding hole until they gave up and left.

"This went on for about three years from 1918. Sometimes he stayed in safe houses around the city. They treated his family very badly, putting his wife and children out on the streets for hours while they ransacked the house. It was a pretty awful existence, but he put it down to the '*impunities of being in the movement.*'"

Born in Sheep's Head in West Cork, FX joined the Irish Volunteers in 1913 and was in F Company First Battalion during the Rising, fighting on Church Street and moving towards the Four Courts towards the end of the week. Deported to Stafford prison, he was released the following June and took a job with the Irish National Aid and Volunteer Dependents' Fund.

The brainchild of Tom Clarke who was shot along with James Connolly and Patrick Pearse on the first day of executions in May 1916, the fund was set up by Clarke's widow Kathleen to help the families of those who'd played their part in the Rising, to help pay for food, clothes, education and so on. Michael Collins was Secretary of the organisation for fifteen months, and FX was Chief Clerk.

"They brought in staggering amounts of money - £50 here, £100 there," says Gareth. "There was one donation of £7,000 from the Irish Emigrants Society. Altogether, they raised between £100,000 and £150,000."

After eighteen months he moved to New Ireland Assurance, which was set up in 1918 in an effort to keep money in the country. He was one of the first agents called on to collect premiums door-to-door.

"This gave him freedom to gather and deliver information for the movement," says Gareth.

The same year he was elected leader of the Rathfarnham branch of the Irish Republican Army. Todd Andrews, then aged eighteen to FX's thirty-two, mentioned the fact in his memoir, *Dublin Made Me*.

"*We got a new company captain*," Andrews wrote, "*an oldish man from Co. Cork called FX Coghlan. Of medium build with a striking face, he spoke quietly in his soft Cork accent. He has no ambitions for glory, possessions or power and is quite unwar-like.*"

"That was the thing with my grandfather," says Gareth. "The fact he is a forgotten hero is largely due to himself. He shied away from publicity, yet he was a very influential man at the time. He was a socialist in his own way, one who didn't believe in owning property, and he treated everybody with respect.

"After all the excitement of the Rising, he worked doggedly to help people who had been part of it. He wrote countless letters on behalf of families who had fallen on hard times, trying to get them work. And he didn't do it lightly – he went out and interviewed those people, to find out more about them, what they were good at, and then wrote to his old colleagues like Todd Andrews, who went on to found Bord na Mona, and Joe McGrath of the Irish Hospital Sweepstakes, recommending them for specific jobs."

FX served as Company Commanding Officer during the War of Independence with the Irish Volunteers and IRA, and rose through the ranks to become 4th Battalion Commanding Officer of the pro-Treaty IRA from March 1922 during the Truce Period, and Commandant in the National Army to the end of the Civil War. He left the Defence Forces in 1924 at the rank of Commandant and returned to work for the Land Commission.

When his first wife, with whom he had six children, died from TB in 1927, he later he married his boss, who was forced to retire due to the marriage bar in place at the time. They went on to have five children, of whom Gareth's mother is the second youngest.

"For me, the Easter Rising was a bloody protest," says Gareth. "Ultimately, if its aim was to overthrow the British, it never had any real hope of succeeding, but what it really achieved was to raise consciousness that a life outside of British rule was possible.

"The message was clear – we could run this country ourselves, make our own mistakes, and do things our way. For that reason alone, the Rising was a momentous occasion and I couldn't be happier at giving Grandad's medals an airing at the centenary commemorations."

The Mendicity Institution is one of Ireland's oldest charities and in 1916, it was serving food to the homeless people of the city, just as it does today, when rebels took over the building and invited its occupants to leave. Declan Costello's grandfather Patrick Kelly was part of the small Mendicity garrison, who came up with unusual ways of holding the fort. Although Declan never met his grandfather in person, he discovered so much about him in his painstaking research that he was able to share Patrick's story with 120 members of the extended family in the local community hall. The gathering was a wonderful example of a family honouring one of their own in this centenary year, a story played out across the country as people accessed public records online and elsewhere and discovered or strengthened their own personal connections with the Rising.

The Valiant Men
of the Mendicity

It was a hard-fought action worthy of the Alamo and other last stands of military history. On Easter Monday 1916, Sean Heuston led the D company of the First Battalion of Irish Volunteers to seize the Mendicity Institution on the south of the Liffey at Usher's Island.

His orders from James Connolly were to engage any British troops coming out of the Royal Barracks, long enough to give Commandant Ned Daly time to build his defences at the Four Courts. This mission was expected to take only a few hours, after which Heuston could withdraw. In the event, he held the building for over two days.

The Mendicity was then, as it is now, a charity set up to feed Dublin's poor and homeless, but both staff and the unfortunates who awaited their only square meal of that day were unceremoniously evacuated at gunpoint while Heuston and his men barricaded the doors and smashed windows to take up their positions.

After they fired their first rifle volley against British troops advancing along the North Quays, their opponents fell back and Heuston decided to hold his position.

"The British command soon realised that this small unit posed a serious threat and surrounded the building," says Declan Costello, whose grandfather Patrick Kelly was among thirteen Volunteers from Swords in north County Dublin sent as reinforcements the next day.

"It was a tiny garrison of only about thirty men fighting up to four hundred Dublin Fusiliers who, as they closed in, started hurling in hand grenades. Imagine their surprise when the Irish rebels caught them and threw them back out!"

At least two of the rebels, Liam Staines and Dick Balfe were seriously injured when the bombs exploded before they had a chance to throw them back out the window. With no food and hopelessly outnumbered by forces equipped with superior ammunition, Heuston surrendered on Wednesday.

"My grandfather was taken to Arbour Hill and court-martialled on May 4th along with his fellow combatants," says Declan. "He was sentenced to death, but this was later commuted to penal servitude.

"As we know, Sean Heuston was executed on May 8th, but Patrick and the others were taken to Arbour Hill and Mountjoy, and later transferred to Dartmoor, Maidstone, Lewis and Pentonville. They were moved from prison to prison, because they caused trouble. They considered themselves prisoners of war and looked for basic human rights, which they didn't get, so they went on hunger strike.

"Having shared jail time with Eamon de Valera and Thomas Ashe, Patrick was released in June 2017, and he smuggled out a poem written by Ashe, which contains the lines:

'Let me carry your Cross for Ireland, Lord, For Ireland weak with tears,

For the aged man of the clouded brow, And the child of tender years;

For the empty homes of her golden plains, For the hopes of her future too,

Let me carry your Cross for Ireland, Lord, For the cause of Roisin Dubh.'

Patrick Kelly married and had six children. He bought a piece of land in Lusk, Co. Dublin, and built a house, a bicycle shop, sweet shop and electrical repair shop.

"He was the first man in the town to have a radio," says Declan. "He'd built it himself and whenever there was an All-Ireland match, he hung a loudspeaker outside the shop and hundreds of men from the neighbouring towns and villages of the Naul, Balbriggan, Donabate and other places nearby gathered in the square listening to it."

Like most of his generation, Patrick did not reminisce with his family about his participation in the Rising, or share

43

information about his detainment at His Majesty's pleasure.

"But my grandmother did tell of one time when she urged him to follow up on a missed payment of his military service pension and his response, though brief, was filled with emotion. 'I didn't go out to fight for a bloody pension!' he said and left the room.

"After my father's funeral in February last year (2014), my cousin Helen Kelly and I started chatting and agreed it was important to get the story of our grandfather together for the family, before it missed another generation and was potentially lost forever.

"Through his pension application and stories from aunts and uncles, we pieced together his life story, including his role in the Rising, and called the 120-strong extended family together in the local community hall, to share this story with them. Patrick died in 1945 and had twenty-three grandchildren, none of whom had got the chance to meet him. I'm now an expert on a man I've never met."

Declan and Helen went to visit the place where their grandfather had fought – and got quite a surprise when they got there.

"There's nothing to mark what happened during the Rising. I contacted the Mendicity Institution, and the HSE, which leases the building on Usher's Island, to see how they'd feel about us putting up a plaque. They said it was no problem.

"We networked through the 1916 Relatives' Association and formed the Mendicity Garrison Relatives Group. The wording will be in English and Irish and it will include the names of each of the combatants. I think that's a fitting tribute to a group of men who fought so valiantly for Irish freedom."

A commemorative plaque and a bronze Roll of Honour were unveiled at the Mendicity Institution in April 2016.

Paddy Holahan produced an impressive digital book about his grandfather's role in the 1916 Rising. Intended as a family record, it's so well crafted, it would be appreciated by anybody with an interest in the period. Aged just eighteen at the time of the Rising, Paddy Hugh Holahan had risen through the ranks of Na Fianna Éireann, Ireland's answer to the Boy Scouts, and like so many of his peers, by the time the Rising took place, he was ready and eager to be in the thick of the action. But how that excitement must have turned to blind terror one night when, in the pitch black darkness of a rooftop posting, he thought every chimney pot was a British soldier. He recalled those moments in a journal that was so colourful and detailed, I suspected his story for the Irish Independent one hundred years later might just write itself.

The Rebellion of 1916
Started with a Game

The most striking aspect of a faded photograph of Na Fianna Éireann from its 1913 Ard Fheis is the cherubic faces of children sitting cross-legged in the front row. There's something incongruous in the sight of boys as young as ten or eleven in military-style uniform flanked by teenagers and adults also in full regalia.

At the centre of the picture is Constance Markievicz, who founded the organisation with Bulmer Hobson in 1909. Also present is one fifteen-year-old First Lieutenant Patrick Hugh Holahan, a boy whose father had served in the British forces yet, at his swearing-in ceremony, Paddy vowed, as did all Na Fianna Éireann boys, "I will never join the British army."

In his recollections written at the age of twenty-five, he

described the Fianna as being "bound together by a simple promise – to work for the independence of Ireland."

But if one man's patriotism is another's brainwashing, Paddy's grandson and namesake today has no illusions about the purpose of the movement.

"Baden-Powell's Boy Scouts indoctrinated empire kids in preparation for joining the British army and Na Fianna Éireann was an antidote to that," he says. "It was set up to feed young men into the Irish forces, and by the time the Rising came about, they were so well drilled, they were well up for it."

They'd already had plenty of practice. In 1914 these boys-to-men, now acting as the Youth Wing of the Irish Volunteers, helped unload and secure almost a thousand rifles and thirty thousand rounds of ammunition from the yacht Asgard as part of the Howth Gun Running operation.

Two years later, on Easter Monday 1916, Paddy was selected as one of a group of Fianna to attack the Magazine Fort in the Phoenix Park to procure weapons, and then blow it up to signal the start of the rebellion.

It started with a game of football. As ordered, the players moved closer to the main gate as the game progressed, then kicked the ball over the gate. When one boy asked permission to get the ball back, the sentry at the gate thought it an innocent request and let him in, but once he opened the gate, the Fianna rushed the sentries and captured them.

They packed rifles and ammunition into a hackney, released their prisoners and while the building didn't explode, they set it on fire, which took days to extinguish. Mission accomplished, they set off for Blackhall Place, and it wasn't just their bicycles that were pumped; the boys were now hungrier than ever for a taste of battle.

Under the command of Ned Daly, Paddy fought in the Four Courts garrison where on his first night he was posted on the roof of a house in North Brunswick Street.

"*I thought every chimney pot was a soldier and I shot at them during the night,*" he wrote.

"*The next morning the Fianna were selected to attack the Broadstone, where the military had taken up position and attacked a party of our men. I was placed in charge of Clarke's Dairy and Sean Laffan in charge of Moore's buildings. On Thursday Laffan was wounded and I was put in charge of both places, although then only eighteen years of age. On Saturday morning we forced the British out of O'Reilly's public house, and Sean Howlett and Paddy Daly were wounded. We kept up a great fight until about 6pm, when rumours of surrender came through. We could not understand that, as we were all right and had lost only one man.*

"*When darkness fell, with all the street and house lights out, there was a complete blackout, during which the nerves of everybody were at their tensest, awaiting the expected attack. Prowling about the dark, deserted rooms, imagination exaggerated things. I entered one room, and was startled to see an armed man confronting me. I challenged and, receiving no reply, fired. The crash of breaking glass brought me to my senses. I had fired at my own reflection in a wardrobe mirror.*

"From dawn on Friday until the end, the attack all over the city became intense. Heavy firing was heard from all directions... When night came, an armoured car appeared and its fifteen occupants jumped out and proceeded to fire into every house along North King Street. The few occupants lay face down in the rooms while bullets pounded the walls over them.

"One soldier, endeavouring to club in a door with the butt end of his rifle, killed his comrade when the rifle went off... It was pitch dark and the only guide to a target was the flash of a rifle. A scream or a groan announced when a bullet had reached its mark."

Such graphic accounts inspired Paddy Hugh's grandson Paddy to chart his grandfather's military career for family posterity in an online book which provides a unique perspective of the Easter Rising through the eyes of someone who took part in it.

"The children of those involved in the Rising will be gone in another twenty years," says Paddy. "The link will be broken. That's why it's so important we hear their stories while we can. These are personal, family stories, but they're also of great value as records of our military history. They're real and honest, and I believe important on many levels, human, historical and political.

"Grandad was aged eighteen to twenty-five between 1916 and 1923, so his growing-up years coincided with the birth of the country."

Paddy Hugh went on to command the 1st Battalion of the Dublin Brigade during the Battle of Dublin in the Civil War.

"The Civil War will be very hard to commemorate," says Paddy. "My grandparents were staunch republicans, while Granny's brother was pro-Treaty and, as was echoed throughout the land, the family was split."

On his release from Frongoch prison in Wales, Paddy Hugh became a trade unionist. He rejoined the army during the Emergency in 1939, when he set up a reserve force with Old IRA men, both pro- and anti-Treaty.

"The reserve force was very symbolic and helped to heal old wounds," says Paddy.

To view a copy of the book, *Patrick Hugh Holahan, Volume One*, visit: http://bit.ly/1Ongptb

Whenever conversation turned to women of the Rising, historian Sinéad McCoole's name consistently popped up, over and over again, until eventually I had a quiet word with the ghosts of mná na hÉireann: 'Okay, I hear you. I will contact her.' What Sinéad doesn't know about the women (and men) of 1916 isn't worth knowing, yet she wears her knowledge lightly and busies herself finding out more about all kinds of women, not just the famous ones. She describes herself as a custodian of their stories, and I can't think of anybody better suited to bringing 'her story' back into history. Ironically, at the time of our chat in September 2015, the news of the day was saturated with controversy over the introduction of gender quotas in an effort to bring more women into Irish politics. Funny, Ireland didn't have that problem a hundred years ago.

The Rise of
Mná na hÉireann

One thing the Irish freedom fighters had no need of in 1916 was gender quotas. Mná na hÉireann at that time rocked the system in their droves, and historian Sinéad McCoole says today's generation would find no better role models than these of our forebears.

Author of several bestselling books focusing on the women of the era, it's hard to think of anyone more qualified to bring these women's stories to life. And now, with the spotlight shining ever more brightly on the Rising, she's training that light on hitherto unknown women to take their place in history as equals to such luminaries as Maud Gonne and Countess Markievicz.

"There were masses of women in politics at the turn of the

Century," says Sinéad. "Many came in through the trade union movement and Inghinidhe na hÉireann (Daughters of Ireland), the forerunner of Cumann na mBan.

"These women were doers; they rolled up their sleeves and made things happen. For some it was a military struggle while others saw it as a humanitarian crisis, some got involved for political reasons and others because they wanted to see cultural change.

"They came from all walks of life. They were shop assistants, doctors, housewives, laundry workers, artists, teachers and even schoolchildren. They were rich and poor, of all religions and none, and many were imprisoned for their beliefs, both in the aftermath of 1916 and the Civil War.

"In 1923, there was the greatest mass arrest of political women ever recorded in Ireland and, while incarcerated, they endured the full rigours of hunger strike and separation from family and friends."

One of those, Teresa O'Connell, contacted Sinéad in 1994 when she was curating an exhibition called *Guns & Chiffon* in Kilmainham Jail.

'*As an ex-prisoner of Kilmainham Jail, I have no records left as things were confiscated,*' she wrote. '*As far as I know, many of my friends there are now happy with God... Thank you very much for remembering Ireland's dead.*'

"Over the next five years, I met with Teresa often," says Sinéad. "As she recounted her memories of those times, she was transformed from an old lady in her nineties to a young girl again. She recited poetry, sang songs and told me about the conditions and lives of her fellow inmates.

"When she attended the launch of the exhibition in 1997, I saw her glancing around the main compound of Kilmainham Jail with a look of nostalgia, as if she could see the laughing, smiling faces of her comrades who had been imprisoned with her almost seventy-five years before."

And then there's the story of Christy Halpin, who started clearing out his Aunt Bridie's New York apartment after her funeral and discovered her secret past. Far from the frail old spinster aunt he remembered, a new figure emerged from the photos, newspaper clippings and jail journal he found in a suitcase under the bed. Jail journal? He read on…

'*Far better the grave of a rebel without cross, without stone, without name, than a treaty with treacherous England that can only bring sorrow and shame. Bridie Halpin, Kilmainham Jail.*'

"Bridie Halpin's story was not unique," says Sinéad. "Many of the women who participated in Ireland's fight for freedom never spoke about this period of their lives, particularly those imprisoned for their part in the Civil War. The bitterness of those years meant that it was an episode best concealed. Also, it was a source of extreme embarrassment to some families that their womenfolk had been in prison."

In her book *Easter Widows*, Sinéad chronicles the lives and loves of the leaders' wives: Lillie Reynolds Connolly, Maud Gonne MacBride, Kathleen Daly Clarke, Áine O'Brennan

Ceannt, Agnes Hickey Mallin, Grace Gifford Plunkett and Muriel Gifford MacDonagh. She also debunks some of the myths about certain events, such as the marriage of Grace with Joseph Mary Plunkett, for instance.

"Some people think they spent his last night together, but in fact, they had only ten minutes with each other after their wedding in Kilmainham Jail, hours before his execution," she says. "Grace said that for two people who'd always had so much to say to each other, in the end, for those precious minutes, supervised by prison guards, they were at a loss for words."

Sinéad felt compelled to write women into Irish history when she saw just how much of their presence was missing.

"As a historian, I see my role as that of custodian of people's stories. And whether it's writing a book or curating an exhibition, it's important to put these stories out there so that people are remembered."

When not writing or curating, Sinéad runs the renowned Jackie Clarke Collection in Ballina, Co. Mayo, a treasure trove of historic memorabilia collected by the eponymous local businessman. An original copy of the Proclamation and a cockade from the hat of Wolfe Tone are among the 100,000 items in the archive.

As a result of projects for 2016, she has had a chance to meet descendants of activists of whom she says, "They're like my extended family. I knew many of them in my twenties and it's great to have the chance to catch up again."

Books by Sinéad McCoole include *Guns & Chiffon: Women Revolutionaries and Kilmainham Jail, 1916-1923; Easter Widows*; and a recently updated edition of her bestseller *No Ordinary Women: Activists in the Revolutionary Years 1900-1923* (O'Brien Press).

Artist Norman Teeling's association with 1916 was established twenty years ago, when his paintings were hung in the GPO to mark the 80th anniversary of the Rising. That they were taken down in 2005 and never put back up raised hackles in certain quarters this year, but Norman merely shrugged his shoulders and produced a sublime new collection. As he talked about what the Rising meant to him, he had me variously howling with laughter, welling with pride and shedding tears of frustration at Ireland's lack of appreciation of the arts, particularly in this centenary year. How shall we commemorate our artistic heritage a century after the cultural revolution that went hand in hand with the Rising? Let's bundle it in with regional development, rural affairs and the Gaeltacht. Hark, what's that spinning sound from the graves of our dead patriots?

'1916 Memories Should be Alive Every Year
- Not Every Hundred Years'

It's twenty years since he was commissioned by An Post to mark the 80th anniversary of the Easter Rising with a series of paintings for the GPO, but as the centenary approaches, his works have long since disappeared from public view.

Now, despite calls for his paintings to be reinstated inside the landmark building, artist Norman Teeling has no intention of entering into the debate. And as far as he is concerned he doesn't need to, because he plans to revisit the Rising with a completely new series of commemorative paintings.

His previous collection was a high point of the 80th anniversary, comprising a series of ten paintings depicting Teeling's interpretation of iconic images such as the wounded James Connolly being comforted by his comrades, a Volunteer raising the flag of the Irish Republic on the rooftop, and Padraig Pearse reading the Proclamation on the steps of the GPO.

Unveiled as part of the 1996 celebrations, the original collection remained on public view in the main hall of the GPO until the building was refurbished in 2005. They were then put into storage where they remain to this day. Now An Post communications director Barney Whelan says the State company is actively seeking a new home for the collection ahead of next year's centenary commemorations.

"The public hall is not a suitable space to house an art collection," he says. "These are large paintings and some jutted out from pillars too narrow to accommodate them. We're storing them very carefully and want to find them a good home. We'd be delighted to hear from somebody who's in a position to display them properly and we'll work with them to ensure the paintings can be seen by the Irish public in a purpose-built setting where they can be viewed at their best."

The artist himself remembers the frantic deadline of the commission in early 1996, which came about almost by chance.

"There wasn't a lot of visual references, because nobody took photos much back in 1916, so I did some research and painted half a dozen pictures of how I imagined the thick of the action in the GPO would have been. Then I left them in the garage where a friend, Brian Sheridan, saw them and asked, 'What are you doing with that lot?' I said I'd been meaning to call the GPO to see if An Post wanted them.

"'No need, I'll do that for you,' said Brian. He had the

cheek to ask and they said yes, the 80th anniversary's coming up – we'll take four and can you do six more in six weeks, in time for the commemorations? I did a painting a week to meet the deadline."

A few months after the launch, Norman came across a group of Americans on a walking tour of Dublin heading for the GPO.

"The tour guide said to them, 'Right, let's do the Stations,' as the collection was commonly known, so I tagged along and stood at the back while he led them to the first of my paintings. He described the scene, then told his customers to study it on their own for a minute, at which point he came over to me and asked me to leave, in no uncertain terms.

"'*Listen here, this is a paying tour – clear off!*' he said.

"I explained I was the painter and, without skipping a beat, he took me by the elbow and announced, '*Get your cameras ready – we have the artist right here!*'"

Norman laughs at the memory as he prepares for his own event to mark the 2016 commemorations.

"It struck me last year that these paintings might not be seen again, so I decided to have my own exhibition at the Oriel Gallery in Dublin. I've already completed a dozen paintings of scenes at the GPO, the Four Courts and other parts of the city, and portraits of the rebel leaders.

"This collection tells a story that's more informed than the first, because I've had more time to immerse myself in the history and characters of the period. And I'm a better painter than I was twenty years ago. I've been influenced by the beauty and poignancy of the arts of that era too. *The Wayfarer* by Pádraig Pearse is a gorgeous poem, and to think he wrote it the night before he was executed is astonishing."

His research into 1916 and the years that followed has proved an education for Norman who, like many of his generation, learned little about this important part of our history at school.

"My mother Maura, who's ninety-seven, tells of her Aunt Brigid regularly wheeling a pram full of guns through town to bring them from one place to another in the lead up to the Rising. I learned more about those times from her than anything I'd been taught at school. History was beaten into us as children and it was all figures and dates. I didn't put it together until I started doing my own research and what an amazing discovery it's been.

"The Easter Rising is the most important event to have happened in this country, yet there's no pride shown in it whatsoever.

"Other countries celebrate their historic events on an annual basis. Look at how the Fourth of July is marked in America, Poppy Day in Britain, Bastille Day in France... It seems to me that other nations honour their history and we don't. It's crazy."

Some might put that down to the struggles we have with parades, particularly those with a record of stirring up sectarian divides, but Norman says it's time to put past hostilities behind us and reclaim our national heritage.

"For a brief period in the 1950s, we did mark the Rising," he points out. "*An Tóstal* was a massive celebration that took place every Easter Sunday. It was better than Paddy's Day, with the biggest floats and the army marching in the biggest parade. And then suddenly, it was dropped from the calendar. I say let's bring back our annual Easter Rising holiday."

Launched in 1953, *An Tóstal* (The Pageant) was a series of festivals held in towns and villages all over the country to attract tourists during the Easter off-season. Having failed to bring in the anticipated business, however, the event died out in 1958, except for Drumshanbo, Co. Leitrim, where it continues to this day.

Norman would like to see a revival of the festival not only to celebrate Irish life and culture, but also to pay tribute to the heroes of 1916. It should be an event for all the people, he adds, not one to be appropriated by political interest groups. Despite being brought up in a staunchly republican household – or perhaps because of it – he says he has no affiliations to any political party.

"In our house, Dev was akin to Jesus Christ. My father was close friends with Charlie Haughey and as a boy, I was brought out canvassing at every election. However, when that kind of thing is stuffed down your throat, you can rebel against it and I grew up preferring to spend my time on art, music and poetry than politics.

"However, Haughey was a man of vision who appreciated art and culture. He brought in the tax exemption for artists, because he used to say nothing survives but art. He encouraged art in all its forms – painting, sculpture, literature, poetry, music, dancing, acting... the lot. Now those tax exemptions are all but eroded and many artists can barely eke out a living.

"I'm okay, I'm seventy-one and I have a pension, but I know other younger men and women who are literally hungry artists, living on beans. Art is dying in this country. It's a terrible indictment considering the cultural, literary and artistic revival that flourished a hundred years ago.

"Our forebears of 1916 got it. They were artists, idealists and dreamers. Who else would have had the vision to orchestrate the Rising? A realist would have said, 'Are you off your rocker?' Yet here were a few brave men and women taking on the might of the British empire, one of the most powerful forces on the planet. It was insane.

"I believe they knew in their hearts it wouldn't work, yet still they were prepared to lay down their lives so the generations that followed might be free.

"The Rising itself was a flop, but it was the spark that lit the bonfire of the ensuing War of Independence and the Civil War. And the 1916 rebels didn't fail because they died; on the contrary, their executions opened the eyes of the Irish people and after that we never gave in.

"These revolutionaries, and Wolfe Tone before them, were inspiring beyond measure. Our freedom wasn't handed to us, we had to fight for it, and they paid the ultimate sacrifice.

"These men are our heroes. There should be a monument

to them on O'Connell Street and a national holiday in their honour. We should keep the memories of these people alive every year, not every hundred years."

The Wayfarer
by Pádraig Pearse

The beauty of the world hath made me sad,
This beauty that will pass;
Sometimes my heart hath shaken with great joy
To see a leaping squirrel in a tree,
Or a red lady-bird upon a stalk,
Or little rabbits in a field at evening,
Lit by a slanting sun,
Or some green hill where shadows drifted by
Some quiet hill where mountainy man hath sown
And soon would reap; near to the gate of Heaven;
Or children with bare feet upon the sands
Of some ebbed sea, or playing on the streets
Of little towns in Connacht,
Things young and happy.
And then my heart hath told me:
These will pass,
Will pass and change, will die and be no more,
Things bright and green, things young and happy;
And I have gone upon my way
Sorrowful.

I'd come across a series of YouTube videos that caught my eye. They featured a whole cross-section of people whose relatives had been active during the Easter Rising, and they were all made by Marcus Howard, a multimedia and business teacher-cum documentary film maker. Unlike some slick productions that value style over substance, I found these videos captivating; they allowed people to tell their stories in their own words and had a natural, unforced, unscripted, authentic quality. I tried several times to find the film maker, but for some strange reason, I hit a brick wall. How hard can it be to contact someone these days? Then by happy coincidence, Marcus emailed me to tell me a little bit about his videos and his own connection with the Rising, I was delighted to hear from him. I couldn't find Marcus, but when the time was right, he found me.

Arrested and Fed Dog Biscuits:
Only the Strongest Survived

Long before John F Kennedy urged Americans to "ask not what your country can do for you – ask what you can do for your country," countless Irish citizens of 1916 were putting their lives on the line for theirs.

Now, thanks to relatives wading through the mists of time to find their own connections with the Rising, local heroes are emerging across the nation to take their place in the annals of history. These were ordinary people, like Arthur Greene, who marched from Dundalk and ended up being thrown in jail and left to sleep on a bare stone floor and fed dog biscuits for his part in the rebellion.

In the weeks leading up to the Rising, Arthur, then a Sergeant Major with the Irish Volunteers, met with his friend

John Kieran in the John Boyle O'Reilly Hall where they moulded lead into bullets. His mother fashioned fabric into haversacks for carrying ammunition and whenever neighbours dropped by to ask, "What are you making?" she'd say, "Aprons for our granddaughters in Glasgow."

On hearing "Dublin is up!" the Dundalk Volunteers collected a cache of rifles in Ardee, then marched sixty miles and took Tyrrellstown House on the outskirts of the capital.

They heard gunfire in the city, but were under orders to hold Tyrrellstown for further notice. Eight days later, on May 1st, word came back that the rebels had been defeated and they'd be surrounded that night by military and RIC. It was time to evacuate.

They walked mostly by night, resting in barns by day. Within an hour of his return home, Arthur was arrested and taken to Richmond Barracks where he was thrown into a room with twenty-five others and given nothing but black tea and dog biscuits for sustenance. Sean McDermott was executed while he was there. A few days later Arthur was released.

"The twelve or fourteen days from when I left town on Easter Sunday 1916 until my return home again were ones of great physical hardship and mental strain," he said in his witness statement. "I will never forget this experience. It took men of great physical endurance to carry on."

Arthur carried on in a different way when, shortly after the Rising his sister Annie died in childbirth, leaving six children, and soon after that her husband also perished. Though Arthur had been engaged for two years, he gave up his fiancée along with his hopes and dreams for a family of his own, to raise his sister's children.

"He saw it as the right thing to do," says his great grand-nephew, Marcus Howard, a multimedia and business teacher and part-time film maker who's posted a series of documentary videos about 1916 on YouTube.

"I don't think we fully appreciate today the enormous personal sacrifice made by people of that era. It must have been terrifying to take on the might of the British empire, but that's what they did. They fought for their country and were an inspiration to countries like India and Russia to rise up in their quest for independence. They deserve to be honoured."

And that's what Marcus is doing, by celebrating these often unsung heroes online. He's now posted seventy-two videos on the YouTube channel Easter Rising Stories and has more in the pipeline. Together they provide an impressive collection of personal stories told by relatives and people with a passion for this extraordinary time in Irish history.

"It's been an education for me," says Marcus. "You learn only so much history at school, but it's a far different thing to walk around Mount Street recalling the story of thirteen men holding up 1,600 British soldiers.

"I also accompanied Donna Cooney as she retraced the steps of her great grand-aunt Elizabeth O'Farrell, the nurse who waved the white flag of surrender from the GPO to Jervis Street.

"The O'Rahilly was an interesting story too, because he was against the Rising at first, and ended up leading the last charge. He was shot on Moore Street and dashed to shelter in a doorway on Sackville Lane, now O'Rahilly Parade."

While he lay dying for over twenty-four hours, the O'Rahilly wrote to his wife on the back of a letter:

Darling Nancy, I was shot leading a rush up Moore Street, took refuge in a doorway. While I was there I heard the men pointing out where I was and I made a bolt for the lane I am in now. I got more than one bullet, I think.

Tons and tons of love dearie to you and the boys and to Nell and Anna. It was a good fight anyhow.

Please deliver this to Nannie O'Rahilly, 40 Herbert Park, Dublin.

Goodbye darling.

In the spirit of 1916, Marcus has made these videos as a not-for-profit educational resource for anybody to see.

"I love the way the series has gone in interesting directions I never planned," he says. "It started when I watched a video about the campaign to save Moore Street, and just evolved from there. Numbers 14 to 17 are to be saved, but the rest of the terrace is currently under threat of demolition.

"Moore Street is such an important landmark, I don't understand how we can take it away from future generations. It's where the rebels retreated after the GPO, the place that saw the signing of the birthplace of the State.

"This is a site of huge historic interest, not to mention a

great tourist location, one which could bring in much-needed jobs. And I say that as a third-level lecturer in business studies. There's great potential to the economy in preserving our heritage."

To view Marcus Howard's videos, visit Easter Rising Stories YouTube channel.

Imagine what the streets of Dublin from the Brazen Head up to the Guinness Brewery were like at a time when this was the industrial heartland of Ireland. John Stephenson did just that, walking the now near derelict quarter, imagining the sounds, smells and colours of a bygone era when it would have been heaving with people, carts, noise and bustling activity. And when the spark of an idea fired his imagination further, he lightened his step. The residents of this historic but frequently forgotten neighbourhood deserved to have something to celebrate, so he started a conversation with other people who could make it happen. My eyes were opened to how one person can engage with an idea, seek out other like-minded souls and together, turn a personal vision into something that enriches a whole community... Remind you of anything?

Bringing the Rising
Back to the Streets

In between tales of *Rob Roy* and *Kidnapped*, John Stephenson's dad captured his son's imagination with bedtime stories of a far more heroic kind. They were John's favourites – tales of his grandfather's real-life adventures in 1916.

Like the day leading up to Holy Week when 21-year-old Quartermaster Paddy Joe (PJ) Stephenson accompanied Michael Staines in moving a cache of rifles and ammunition to Inchicore on a pony and cart. Staines told the driver to turn left at the Old Man's House, occupied by the British Army, and past the sentries at John's Road gate.

'For God's sake Michael, are you out of your mind?" said the driver. 'We'll be pinched, guns and all. Don't you know this place is lousy with Tommies?'

Staines replied, 'Go on, smile, and drive past those soldiers as if you were going to the Strawberry Beds at Lucan.'

When they reached their destination, he grinned and said, 'What did I tell you – the more openly you do it the less you'll be suspected.'

John and his brother held their breath and begged for more. Well then, continued their father, Noel, on Easter Monday, PJ and his peers in D Company of the 1st Battalion of the Irish Volunteers, thinking they were on a route march, came to a sudden halt outside the Mendicity Institution when Commandant Seán Heuston turned right about, faced his men and shouted, 'Company left wheel, seize this building and hold it in the name of the Irish Republic.'

'*At once our pent-up feelings of bewilderment and frustration sought relief in yells and cheers and with a wild rush, we went in through the open gates, up the stone steps and in the front door*,' wrote Paddy Joe in his lyrical and detailed recollections of 1916, a legacy the family treasures to this day.

In his account he describes standing by the window inside the Mendicity building and seeing '*the round top of the helmet of the first Tommy as he jumped across the front gate like a rabbit*,' followed by many more.

'*How many of those rabbits hopped across that opening I could not tell. They seemed to be innumerable.*'

The following night, PJ and Seán MacLoughlin were ordered to go to the GPO, report to Connolly and bring back food for the hungry garrison. Before they returned, however, the Mendicity was surrounded and Heuston had surrendered.

Fast forward seventy-five years and John, PJ's grandson (and nephew of the acclaimed architect Sam Stephenson) was at the forefront of the commemorations of 1991. An arts organiser by profession, he then mobilised Dublin Bus-sponsored 'poet mobiles' to take people on a tour of key garrison points around the city, with readings of works by poets of 1916.

The current President Michael D Higgins, along with Anthony Cronin, Eilís Dillon, Brendan Kennelly and others read their own works at the GPO and in the evening the Chieftains, Hothouse Flowers, Donal Lunny and other musicians performed at Kilmainham Gaol. The event took a huge amount of time and effort to organise and, though the happy memories linger still, John decided to take things a little easier for the centenary. At least, that was the plan.

"I thought I'd keep it simple, just focus on where my grandfather fought," he says. "I wanted to get a feel for the place, so I walked around the area on a kind of reconnaissance – and couldn't find it. I asked a passer-by for directions to the Mendicity Institution.

'What happens there?' he asked.

'They feed the homeless,' I replied.

'Ah, de Mendo!' he said and pointed me right to it.

"For an area that was once the industrial hub of Ireland, with distilling, brewing and linen manufacture all along the stretch from the Brazen Head up to the Guinness Brewery, it's very run-down now. I thought, a hundred years on, is this the best we can do? What have the people who live here got to celebrate?"

Through networking in the relatives' association, John joined others in forming the Mendicity Garrison Relatives Group, which has traced descendants of combatants and got permission to erect a plaque in their honour. But John wanted to do more.

"We can't simply put up a plaque and walk away," he says. "These residents have a rich history and heritage; they shouldn't have to walk through a derelict site. I couldn't not rise to the occasion, so I contacted local service providers and other interested parties, and we're planning a major community-based project involving a garrison re-enactment, installations, cultural and arts events and lots of exciting stuff that I hope will reintroduce the history of this area as a point of pride to those who live here.

"When the fifty-year anniversary of the Rising was marked in 1966, I was fifteen and full of the romantic notion of the heroism and patriotism of the whole thing, but nobody involved the ordinary rank-and-file relatives back then, only those of the leaders. Yet over 2,500 people took part." (The official figure is 2,558 on the rebel side, according to the Military Pensions Archive).

"We were ignored for two generations, but now we're finally getting recognition and being consulted, and there's a great sense of solidarity among all the groups involved.

"For me, the Easter Rising was the founding moment in our modern history and it's important not to lose sight of it, because it's only in learning from our past that we can reimagine our future."

Only two years old when his father Michael Mallin was executed, Father Joseph Mallin was now the only surviving child of any of the rebel leaders. He lives in China, so I contacted his order, the Jesuits. Would he agree to be interviewed? Could I call him? They printed out my email and showed it to him. "I am very hard of hearing," he replied. "A telephone conversation would be unsatisfactory. I could answer by pen if I have an address." His 102nd birthday was coming up on September 13th, so I sent him a card and a letter with fifteen questions. A month later, a letter arrived from Wah Yan College in Hong Kong. 'Dear Ms Naughton, I shall answer your questions first and add some observations. I thank you for your good wishes. Post here is rather erratic; two weeks is pretty average...' Three pages front and back in his own careful handwriting: a letter to treasure.

'My Mother Didn't Burden Us
with Loss and Sorrow'

On the night of May 7th 1916, Agnes Hickey Mallin, five months pregnant and with her oldest three children by her side and the youngest, two-year-old Joseph asleep in her arms, was escorted to her husband's cell in Kilmainham Jail. It was time to say goodbye. It was said that visitors in an adjoining cell heard the Mallin family weeping loudly as they said their final farewells.

Before Agnes and the children left, Michael pressed his last letter to his beloved family into his wife's hand. In it he wrote, '*Una, my little one, be a nun... Joseph, my little man, be a priest if you can.*'

Between 3.45 and 4.05 the following morning Commandant Michael Mallin, second in command of the Irish Citizen Army during Easter Week 1916, was taken out to the Stonebreaker's Yard and shot.

Una did indeed become a Loreto nun and the 'little man' Joseph followed his older brother Seán into the Jesuit order where he's been a priest and teacher for over eighty years. Now 102, Fr Joseph Mallin is the last surviving child of any of the leaders of the Easter Rising.

"This does not place me in any special category," he writes from his home in Hong Kong where he's lived for more than sixty years. Although happy to be interviewed for the *Irish Independent's My 1916* series, his hearing is not what it used to be, so he declines a phone call. Can we write to each other instead, he asks.

I write that very day, asking how much he knew of his father growing up. Did his mother tell him about the handsome man she'd met at seventeen, before he was posted as a British soldier to India for seven years? How they married on his return, by which time his political beliefs had changed profoundly and he joined the rebels fighting the British? Did she proudly recall how Michael became Chief of Staff and second in command to James Connolly in the Irish Citizen Army, and during the Rising led a battalion in St Stephen's Green?

"Quite wisely, my mother did not talk much about my father," says Fr Joseph. "Rather she let me become aware as I grew up. She did not want to burden us with her sense of loss and deep sorrow. Maybe to do so would have been too difficult for her. Her own father had died when she was nineteen years old. He was a Fenian, and exiled, and active in 1867."

So Joseph learned gradually about the father he never knew, from family, friends and historical records. And while there was much to be proud of, there were also questions, one in particular that raised some controversy.

At his court martial on May 5th 1916, Michael Mallin claimed in his defence that he had no knowledge of the Rising and that on his arrival at St Stephen's Green, Countess Markievicz ordered him to take charge of the garrison there. This was untrue. Markievicz had, in fact, been his deputy.

Mallin was reportedly inconsolable that, in his words, "I have left my wife and children absolutely destitute."

Was this his primary motivation in trying to mislead the court martial?

"The nurse Cavell's execution had become public," says Fr Joe, referring to the German execution of the British nurse Edith Cavell in October 1915. That a woman was executed was portrayed around the world as one of the key atrocities of the Great War, giving Mallin reason to believe the British would not shoot a woman. But was taking such a gamble the honourable thing to do? Fr Joe can only imagine the questions that must have weighed heavy on his father's mind.

"Could he leave a family of very young children to destitution? Where did his duty lie? Should he risk putting another in peril in his efforts towards his family?"

Michael Mallin's fears were realised when, after his

execution, Agnes struggled to raise her children in poverty, relying on the support of family and friends to keep them in food and shelter. As a result, Fr Joseph refers repeatedly to his family being 'scattered.'

"Those early years were a time of much unrest. Both sides of our family were involved. These things – ambushes, hold-ups, curfews, raids etc – were part of our days and nights. My mother protected us as best she could. We were destitute, and that scattered us while growing up, but then she had me and my younger sister to care for."

They received great support from Margaret Pearse, sister of Padraig; she ran St Enda's school in Rathfarnham, where Joseph was educated.

"Miss Pearse was of great assistance to us, but does not appear in any public records. There were others, of course. They did not seek recognition, nor did she."

He insists he did not join the clergy out of a sense of duty – "we were never compelled" – and will mark the centenary of his father's execution on May 8th next as he has done every year since becoming a priest.

"As heretofore, I shall set aside Mass for my father."

And while he has no plans for Easter 2016 – "I do not plan my day, nor Easter" – he has thought deeply about what the Rising means to him.

"I'm not sure how to answer this question. I could take it – what was the point in fighting for the freedom to choose which way we would use that freedom? Our free will is not to choose what we would like to do, but what we ought to do. The two can be the same in some cases.

"It meant I would meet many who had by their actions shown unselfishness, even though they lost out thereby. I did meet many such people in 1966."

He's been home a few times since the 50th commemorations, most recently in 2009, when he visited Kilmainham Jail and wryly remarked upon admission, "The first time I came here, I didn't have to pay an entrance fee."

The people of Longford in the heart of the midlands are proud of one of their own. Qualified for some years as a medical doctor, Laura Doherty was on her way to a job interview when she was involved in a road collision that very nearly cost her her life. Recovery was long, slow and put the pain into painstaking, but throughout it all, she demonstrated a determination and resilience that won her renewed respect from those who knew her and knew of her. During that time, she honed her talents as an artist and this year, she illustrated a special centenary calendar with her portraits of the Rising leaders. When I spoke to her about the project, she made it clear just what an inspiration the rebels of 1916 were to her. Yet, as County Librarian Mary Reynolds pointed out, 'Laura speaks of their bravery and idealism, yet she embodies those very qualities herself.'

'The Bravery of the Rising Leaders
Sparked My Passion for Painting'

Doctors didn't expect Dr Laura Doherty to survive the horrific injuries she sustained in a car crash, but like the leaders of the Easter Rising, she battled against incredible odds – and this fight ended in a resounding victory.

Now the 35-year-old Longford woman is using her artistic talents to pay tribute to her heroes with a special calendar featuring her portraits of the 1916 leaders, published as part of the Longford centenary commemorations.

Laura has come a long way since that fateful day in February 2009 when, as a 28-year-old doctor, she was involved in a near fatal accident while on her way to an interview in Sligo where she'd hoped to work as a GP. The collision happened about eight miles from her family home where her parents John and Patricia received the devastating news.

"She was in a coma for ten days and doctors told us to prepare for the worst," recalls her mother Patricia. "It was a terrible time. The whole family was in shock, but we vowed not to leave her on her own for a minute.

"As each day passed by, the doctors grew less hopeful for her recovery, but then one night when her sisters Aoife and Orlaith sat by her side, they started singing softly to her. '*Sonny, don't go away…*'

"Suddenly, Laura opened her eyes. They couldn't believe it! She didn't speak for two months, but then, out of the blue one day, she turned to her brother Patrick and asked, 'What time is it?'"

It was the start of a slow, painstaking recovery during which Laura spent eight months in the National Rehabilitation Hospital learning to walk again and do all the everyday things most people take for granted. Now she goes to the gym three times a week, and while she may not be the athlete she once was – she played football and basketball, and ran a marathon and several half-marathons – she's lost none of her lust for life.

"I lost my career and the ability to play sport, so my hopes and ambitions had to change radically," she says.

During this time, Laura turned to art, something she'd always enjoyed, and as her talent emerged, she became an accomplished portrait artist. Her depictions of the signatories to the Proclamation and other key figures from 1916 were inspired by her newfound interest in the Rising.

"In researching the project, I discovered a part of history that I hadn't known much about," she says. "I came to realise how brave, selfless and idealistic these men and women were, each with their own fascinating story and each bringing a level of integrity, idealism and selfless dedication to the cause of Irish freedom.

"I feel especially proud to be Irish and to say that these are the people who laid the foundations for our independence. They gave their lives for their country and worked so hard to pave the way for our freedom. I don't think any country could lay claim to more honourable and idealistic men and women that we have the privilege of remembering and honouring in 2016."

Laura's calendar forms part of an extensive programme of centenary commemoration activities in her home county. Co-ordinated by County Librarian Mary Reynolds, the programme was launched in November 2015 after almost a year of planning.

"Laura has made an important contribution to our county and produced something of great value to people nationwide," says Mary. "She talks of the bravery and idealism of those who fought in 1916, yet she embodies those very qualities herself. She's an exceptional woman and we're blessed to have her in our community.

"She spoke beautifully at our launch, as did 16-year-old Transition Year student Adam Farrell, who said, 'It took the burning of our cathedral to show us what Longford working together could accomplish. Even during the recession, our small community was able to band together just like a hundred years ago and make our lives better.'

Completely destroyed by fire on Christmas Day 2008, St Mel's Cathedral in Longford was re-opened in December 2014.

"It rose like the Phoenix from the ashes, and is a monument to the fantastic community spirit we have in Longford," says Mary. "And that's what the centenary commemorations are all about – community.

"This year is an opportunity for every man, woman and child to have a better understanding of the birth of our nation and the people involved – not just the signatories to the Proclamation, but the unsung heroes who took part in the Rising. We know of fourteen from Longford, including Dr Brigid Lyons, then a 20-year-old medical student who tended the wounded in the Four Courts and was later imprisoned in Kilmainham Jail.

"In April we'll have a civic reception for her relatives and those of all the Longford people who participated in the Rising. We'll also have a parade, followed by a reading of the Proclamation.

"There are tons of things going on in our schools, with céilís, debates through Irish, creative writing projects, an original drama in our Youth Theatre, and a cross-border initiative to celebrate everybody who has worked for peace in the land.

"Cultural events include 1916-inspired themes in the Edgeworth and Goldsmith Literary Festivals and the Cruthú

Arts Festival, and there's a time-travel family day on May 6th in Ardagh. GAA clubs from overseas will join Longford GAA for an event at Pearse Park, and there are lots of events planned for the diaspora communities overseas.

"The centenary commemorations rely on people with enthusiasm and commitment and we have that in spades here in Longford."

I'd been itching to meet Donna Cooney ever since seeing her video with Marcus Howard on YouTube. In it, she retraces the steps of her great grand aunt, Elizabeth O'Farrell, the plucky nurse who famously waved the white flag of surrender after the Rising. I spotted her one evening at the launch of 'Portraits and Lives' at the RIA, and took the opportunity to introduce myself and get her number. She was accompanied by Honor O'Brolchain, who also grabbed my interest with anecdotes about her relative, Joseph Mary Plunkett, but more of her anon... I discovered that not only was Donna actively involved in the 1916 Relatives Association and the Save Moore Street campaign, she's also an artist, mother, community activist and keen environmentalist; a few days after our interview, she was heading to Paris for climate talks. I imagine Elizabeth would have been proud.

Sisters in Arms
During the Rising

It was one of the most dramatic moments of the Easter Rising when Nurse Elizabeth O'Farrell waved the flag of surrender that brought the rebellion to an end. According to her great grand niece, Donna Cooney, that's only part of the story.

When Pádraig Pearse decided to evacuate the women from the GPO for their own safety after a week of heavy fighting, Elizabeth, along with Winifred Carney and Julia Grenan, refused to leave. They tended to the wounded there and during their retreat to Moore Lane with "bullets raining from all quarters," according to her own witness statement.

She cooked for the Volunteers who burrowed through the night from house to house, and when Pearse could see the fight was over, Elizabeth was chosen to request talks between the rebels and the British. And later, as agreed with Pearse and General William Lowe, commander of the British forces, it was she who delivered the order to surrender to rebel commands around the city.

In return for her co-operation, Lowe promised she would not be imprisoned and appointed an officer to drive her to the various garrisons. En route to Boland's Mill, however, the driver left her at Butt Bridge, claiming it was unsafe to go any further, so Elizabeth set off alone with no protection from the gunfire whistling all about her.

"I had to take my life in my hands several times," she said. At one point she described the military lined across the top of buildings "screaming at me to go back, but I kept on waving my white flag and the paper."

And when she finally reached her destination, DeValera refused to accept the order from anyone other than his superior officer, Commandant MacDonagh.

Elizabeth set off for Jacob's factory to deliver the message to MacDonagh. While there, two Volunteers asked her to bring £3 in silver to their mother, and another entrusted her with £13 he'd saved to get married. The next morning, Elizabeth's coat was taken, the money confiscated, and she was marched to Kilmainham Jail as a prisoner.

But Elizabeth was not one to take such matters lying down. Outraged, she informed prison officers that, when released, she would "publish to the ends of the earth how General Lowe kept his word of honour."

Lowe apologised the following day for the mistake and, while many in the same circumstances might consider themselves lucky to walk free, the bold Elizabeth asked, "What about the money that was taken from me? There was £16 taken out of my pocket."

Lowe ordered the officer to return the money immediately and Elizabeth went on her way, reporting later that she found General Lowe "most courteous."

After the Rising she became a midwife in Holles Street, opened her own nursing home and died in 1957 at the age of seventy-two. She never married and is buried in Glasnevin Cemetery along with her lifelong friend Julia Grenan, which has led some to wonder if the pair's relationship was more than one of friendship.

"I don't think so," says her great grand niece, Donna Cooney. "Elizabeth had been engaged to an engineer, but he took a job abroad and she didn't want to leave her beloved country. She devoted herself to Ireland instead of having a family of her own.

"She and Julia had been to school together, both became nurses, and during the Rising, they witnessed people being shot all around them. That leaves an indelible mark. These days soldiers are offered counselling to deal with post-traumatic stress, but these were different times.

"Elizabeth and Julia experienced the horrors of war together. They were sisters in arms. It must have been therapeutic for them to be able to confide in each other and not bottle it up for the rest of their lives."

Donna is extremely proud of her plucky great grand aunt, whose indomitable role in the Rising is celebrated by the entire extended family.

"I come from a long line of strong women," she says. "We grew up believing we could do and be whatever we wanted, just as Elizabeth did."

Elizabeth became disillusioned by successive Irish governments, however, none of whom she felt delivered the equality for women that had been promised in the Proclamation.

"Once all the fighting was over and the Treaty accepted, Irish women were pretty much sent back to the kitchen and told to forget about equal status. That was not what Cumann na mBan had expected or fought for."

Donna is determined to celebrate the contribution made by all the women and men who rose for Irish freedom. As PRO for the 1916 Relatives Association, a voluntary group of over 1,700 members and growing by the day, she's busy planning events and working with many other centenary commemoration bodies. She's also involved with the Save Moore Street campaign.

"The Government bought Numbers 14 to 17 Moore Street, but the rest was in the care of NAMA who sold to developers. The Save Moore Street campaign hopes to raise enough money, both here and with the diaspora, to buy the properties back and protect the entire terrace. This is the scene of the surrender, an urban battlefield site of exceptional historical significance and the OPW would do an excellent job of preserving it.

"We're realistic about time frames – this is not something to be done for next year, but to have a workable plan in place, with funding put aside for estimates each year… that would be a wonderful legacy to leave behind for future generations."

For further information visit www.1916relatives.com

If the 'My 1916' series was to be inclusive, it was time to travel northwards and see what stories might unfold there. The National Treasure put me on to Ballymoney Museum manager Keith Beattie, who in turn told me about Maureen Waugh, granddaughter of Gerald Hoy, one of three internees Roger Casement managed to have released from a German prisoner of war camp. Having delved into her family history in recent times, Maureen, who lives in Leicester in England, uncovered some big surprises. My education was broadened as she regaled me with a remarkable personal story intertwined with events in Europe during World War One, filled with a variety of characters - some duplicitous and self-serving, some noble and heroic, others somewhere in between... Maureen, you could write a book about it. Go on, say you will.

'I Hope I've Restored My Grandfather's Reputation'

When Maureen Waugh set out to trace the history of her grandfather in recent times, she uncovered a dark secret the family had concealed for decades.

Gerald Hoy from Dungannon, Co. Tyrone was said to have betrayed Roger Casement, the Irish Republican who had secured his release from a German prison camp while recruiting volunteers for the Easter Rising. To Hoy's staunchly Nationalist family, this was an act so treacherous, his name was never mentioned again. But now his granddaughter wants to put the record straight.

A language teacher living in Berlin with his German wife and their two children, Gerald Hoy was one of 4,000 British nationals rounded up and interned in Ruhleben racecourse at the outbreak of the First World War.

"Conditions in the camp were appalling," says Maureen. "They kept the men in horseboxes ten feet square by ten feet high, six men per stall. Others, like my grandfather, were put in haylofts overhead, hopelessly overcrowded with barely space to stand upright."

It was here Gerald met an old schoolfriend, John Bradshaw from Ballymoney, Co. Antrim, and William Coyne, a law student from Mayo. Following interventions by Sir Roger Casement, these and three other internees were released on grounds of 'ill health,' something the British doubted. Their suspicions were valid – in his letters to German officials, Casement wrote of his intent to exploit the three men to his political advantage back in Ireland. Overall, however, his attempts to recruit Irish volunteers from PoW camps in Germany ended in failure.

"Casement made a lot of strategic errors," says Maureen. "His PR was poor, for a start. He arrived at these camps with a German chauffeur, when at the time, the vast majority of Irishmen were anti-German. He misjudged the strength of Irish loyalty."

But Hoy, Bradshaw and Coyne were impressed by Casement's visit.

"Coyne wrote to him on February 15th 1915 to the effect that 'Ireland has no quarrel with Germany, and we support your belief that Ireland should be an independent state,'" says Maureen. "He went on to ask Casement to 'use your great influence to secure our release and permission to return to Ireland.'"

The following month the three were released. Bradshaw and Coyne went home to Ireland and Gerald joined his wife Luise Kaufmann Hoy in England.

"My grandmother had been left destitute. As she'd married a British national she was ineligible for welfare in Germany. She had to rely on the kindness of her sister and sister-in-law to share their meagre rations with her. Then in January 1915, Sir Edward Grey negotiated for the wives and children of internees to be deported to England. Luise went to Preston, Lancashire.

"My grandfather's uncle, Hugh Cleland Hoy, worked as a secretary at the Admiralty, where British Naval Intelligence was based. They knew Roger Casement was involved in planning an uprising and, keen to impress his superiors, Hugh thought he'd get some intelligence on Casement from his young nephew.

"Gerald had a dilemma: he had no money, and he had to look after his wife and family, so where did his loyalties lie? It wasn't as if it was a stranger talking to him, it was an uncle who said he'd help him out financially if he'd tell him what he knew.

"In truth, Gerald knew very little, so he made stuff up. He said he was the main person to approach Casement, even though it was Coyne who'd made the initial move. He said he'd visited Casement in his hotel, yet he'd never even met the man. He gave Casement's alias and address in Berlin, but these were already known to the authorities as they'd been intercepting his mail since 1914. So what he said in his five-page statement wasn't worth a hill of beans."

Hugh Cleland Hoy made the betrayal claims public in a book he wrote in the 1930s.

"I was eight when my grandfather died. My father wouldn't speak his name, and then four decades later I discovered why – he was ashamed of him! Gerald was no saint, the family knew that. But even though he was a womaniser and a poor provider, this perceived betrayal of Casement was considered the worst offence of all. It was unforgivable.

"From what I can gather, my grandfather was a clever, articulate and charming man, but those qualities hid a weak character. However, Hugh Cleland misrepresented him; he persuaded him to make a statement and exaggerated what he had to tell. By putting the story in context, I hope I've managed to reinstate his reputation in the family to some extent."

Hanged for treason in London's Pentonville Prison in August 1916, Casement was the only Rising leader to be executed outside Ireland.

"Casement knew the Rising was a lost cause, and returned to Ireland to try to prevent it," says Maureen. "However, even though the Rising failed, the British chose to martyr its leaders and martyrs bring recruits, just as they do to this day.

"To me the Rising was a tragic event, but it paved the way for negotiations to start up again with the Treaty. I don't agree with partition, but at least it was some kind of solution. I think

Ireland should be one island independent of mainland Britain, but that's for another day.

"The peace process in Northern Ireland showed how much can be achieved when people talk, negotiate and resolve things diplomatically."

WHPR, one of the biggest public relations firms in Ireland, emailed me. The account director was working on the redevelopment of Richmond Barracks on behalf of Dublin City Council's centenary programme. The restored exhibition centre there is now a popular tourist attraction. A hundred years ago, however, it was where over 3,000 suspected Easter Rising rebels were held before their sentencing. Some seventy-seven women prisoners involved in the Rising were interned there, among them one Jennie Shanahan, a great grand aunt of singer Damien Dempsey. Would I be interested in talking to Damien for 'My 1916'? "He's very interested in this period of history and his family involvement," said the PR exec. Are you kidding me? It's Damien Dempsey! Of course I'm interested. How soon can we set it up?

'Aunt Jennie Deserves a Song'
- Damien Dempsey

Singer/songwriter Damien Dempsey is so inspired by the activities of his great grand aunt during the Easter Rising, he's written a song about her.

Aunt Jennie is a tribute to Jane (Jennie) Shanahan, a trade union activist, member of the Irish Women Workers Union and a key figure in the Irish Citizen Army. The popular balladeer discovered her almost by chance just a few months ago and was moved to pay his respects by immortalising her in music.

"I was searching online to see if any of my ancestors had been involved in the Easter Rising, when my father said, 'Look for your great grandfather's sister, Jennie Shanahan. She was active in 1916.' Sure enough, there she was, and as I read about her, the hairs on the back of my head stood up."

Jennie Shanahan joined the Irish Citizen Army in 1913, taking part in army manoeuvres and training recruits. In the weeks leading up to the Rising she worked long hours, often bedding down on a pile of overcoats in Liberty Hall to snatch a few hours' sleep.

On Easter Monday, she joined the garrison under the command of Sean Connolly sent to take Dublin Castle. When they failed to do so, they retreated to City Hall. On the way, she met some British soldiers who mistook her for a civilian and asked if she'd been badly treated by the rebels.

'Oh no, Sir,' she replied. 'They treated me well enough, but there must be hundreds of them up there on the roof.'

Believing her, the soldiers advanced cautiously, giving the garrison of only twenty time to regroup. They held City Hall for the next twenty-four hours, thanks largely to Jennie's quick thinking.

Jennie was on the roof with Dr Kathleen Lynn when they saw Sean Connolly walk towards them, then fall dead from a sniper's bullet from the Castle.

After their surrender, the rebels were arrested and taken to Ship Street where, according to Jennie's account, they were held for a week in 'squalid conditions' before being moved to Richmond Barracks.

Jennie was one of more than 3,000 rebels detained there, as was Ned Bridgeman, Damien's great grandfather, who fought in Ned Daly's 1st Battalion in the Four Courts. Ned was sent to Frongoch Prison in Wales, while Jennie was taken to

Kilmainham Jail. She was released on May 8th, the day Michael Mallin was executed.

"She was only in her mid-twenties when all this was going on, and she was fearless," says Damien. "Jennie Shanahan was a proper hardcore warrior. She was from a one-room tenement in Mercer Street and had seen five of her sisters and brothers die in the Third World conditions of the tenements at the turn of the last century.

"People like her give me strength to get involved and make a difference. That's why I joined a recent protest about the water charges, when I was spurred to jump on stage and sing *James Connolly* to connect with that sense of people coming together and standing up for themselves. It was a moving moment. I felt Jennie could have been there with me.

"The signatories of the 1916 Proclamation were a mixture of poets, philosophers and pragmatists with great ideas for the future. Their grandparents would have lived through the famine, or the Irish holocaust, as many people now call it.

"That generation saw their people starve to death in this land that was known as the 'Garden of England,' with every type of food being shipped under armed guard to English ports as millions starved. In my opinion, the Irish holocaust was the reason the Fenians rose and the 1916 Rising happened."

Following her release from prison, Jennie went on to run a hospital at Cullenswood House, where Padraig Pearse had founded St Enda's school. During the War of Independence, she supported the Volunteers and her house was regularly used for sending and receiving despatches.

"She had to hide out in friends' houses to avoid capture by the notorious Black and Tans, who made several attempts to arrest her," says Damien.

"My Granny told me her mother and aunt would get her and all her brothers and sisters into the bed on top of the guns if the British Army or the Tans came into the area.

"When she died in 1936, her coffin was draped in the Starry Plough, the flag of the ICA, and her friend Helena Molony delivered an oration at her graveside in Glasnevin Cemetery. When I think of all she did for this country, I couldn't be more proud, and I wanted to show my respect for her the best way I know how. She deserves a song."

With music by John Colbert, great grandnephew of Con Colbert, one of the executed Rising leaders, the song formed part of Damien's repertoire at commemoration performances in New York, London and Dublin. He also sang it at the re-opening of Richmond Barracks in May 2016.

Richmond Barracks was handed over to the Free State Army in 1922 and became a landmark of working class Dublin. A council housing estate was built there in 1924, and it was also home to a Christian Brothers school until 2007. Now it's an interactive multimedia tourist attraction.

Damien had been to the Barracks before, as well as Kilmainham Jail and other key sites of the rebellion, but now his visits are a very different experience. This time it's personal.

"Discovering my family's connection with the Rising has

given me a new perspective," he says. "I love going back to these places – and now I know who to look out for."

Aunt Jennie by Damien Dempsey is one of the songs featured on the album, *Rising*, by Black Bank Folk.

Emeritus Professor of Economic and Social History at Queen's University Belfast, Liam Kennedy has a brilliant mind and he's not afraid to speak it. As fervour was mounting nationwide in the build-up to the Easter commemorations, his sounded like a lone voice, declaring that we should look back in anger, not with sentimentality, at the 1916 Rising. I was excited by his contribution, not only for his challenging perspective, but because of the substance, conviction and eloquence of his searing logic. Whether you agree with him or not, Liam is an intellectual giant who boldly questions established viewpoints and is not afraid to challenge the sacred cows of Irish history. This from his own Research Statement: "In his darker moments he contests the notion of the MOPE syndrome: that in the comparative historical stakes the Irish were the Most Oppressed People Ever."

'The Proclamation is Fanciful, Evasive and Presumptuous'

My introduction to the Easter Rising was in a two-teacher national school in Ileigh, Co Tipperary in the 1950s. There were forty-three pupils in the entire school, with four or five classes in the same teaching room. Graduating into the senior cycle was like entering the Republic of Fear.

Our teacher was utterly devoted to Catholicism, the Irish language and Patrick Pearse. They seemed to form a sacred trinity, a faith and fatherland complex as it were. He was also devoted to *an bata* (the stick), and because he was overweight, his beatings were usually accompanied by angry grunts.

Possibly influenced by the IRA campaign of the late 1950s but more likely because of his passion for Pearse, he had us older boys drilling in the school yard. He often spoke to us of

St Enda's as a model for Irish schooling, with its emphasis on heroism, athleticism and our native language. Only much later did I come to realise that St Enda's was a rather creepy place burdened with latently paedophilic tensions. In any case we learned how to stand to attention, turn smartly – *ar dheis, ar chlé* – and march in the manner of boy soldiers.

My pictorial image of the 1916 Rising was from an illustrated history of Ireland published by the Christian Brothers. This showed the GPO in flames with a profile of Pearse in heroic pose. His bad eye was forever turned away from history.

There is a family story that one of my grand uncles owned a Dublin pub that was looted during the early days of the Rising. Not only that, some of the looters came back afterwards to complain that the whiskey was watered down. They hadn't realised the large bottle of Power's in the window was for display purposes and contained only coloured water. Be that as it may, my embryonic socialist feeling was that the tenement dwellers of Dublin deserved a bit of cheer, once in a lifetime at least.

Perhaps these were the unblemished heroes of 1916. Unlike the British troops and the Irish insurrectionists, they had no innocent blood on their hands.

Despite some gathering doubts about the Rising during my student days, I regarded the Proclamation of the Irish Republic as an iconic text, to be revered rather than analysed. Down the years I have heard it read in graveyards and at political meetings. When I was given floor space in a flat in Montreal by a fellow Irishman in 1967- this was during the World Fair, Expo '67 – I was pleased to see he had a postcard-sized version of the Proclamation on his mantelpiece. (He also had eye-arresting, Playboy centrefold spreads plastered on his bathroom walls).

To my shame, it was only in recent years that I finally got round to reading the Proclamation with some care. The text is disappointing, to say the least. It is fanciful, evasive and incredibly presumptuous. I hadn't noticed the vainglorious and make-believe character of it all.

A small, unrepresentative bunch of fanatical nationalists, none of whom had been elected, presumed to speak on behalf of the Irish people and plunge them, without so much as a by-your-leave, into the most terrible of all states, that of war and its associated terrors.

Who suffered most? Not the insurgents; fewer than a hundred were killed, some at the hands of their own inexperienced comrades. Not the British army, you can be sure. It was the plain people of inner-city Dublin who died in their hundreds to satisfy the blood-drenched fantasies of a group of less-than-impressive poets and marginal figures on the Irish political scene.

The consequences of this act of propaganda are with us to this day. Think of the Provisional IRA whose actions were authored by the Proclamation. A large mural in north Belfast shows the late Martin Meehan, a leading IRA man, crouching in firing position, with the text of the 1916 Proclamation in the background. Think of the dissident IRA who also claim the mantle of 1916.

Easter 1916 was a pivotal moment in Irish history. It copper-fastened Partition and deformed Irish politics. How could fellow Irish people of a unionist persuasion, who made up a quarter of the population, even think of an all-Ireland state after an insurrection that proudly proclaimed its alliance with the armies of the German Kaiser? Despite some progressive rhetoric, the Rising ensured that concern with social inequality and individual liberties was effectively sidelined, North and South, for generations.

It is vitally important to commemorate Easter 1916, but not in the triumphalist manner of the 50th anniversary in 1966. The more discussion the better, but we should leave celebration to *X-Factor* contestants.

We owe it to 'the men of 1916' to look seriously and dispassionately at what they stood for and the flow of events following Easter Monday. This means facing up to the malign consequences that ensued: deep political divisions within nationalist Ireland, the emergence of a Northern Ireland statelet, and a tradition of green jingoism that is still with us.

If we must have heroes, there are better role models than 'the men of 1916' (and yes, there were women too). There are our great writers, from Joyce to Banville, and from Yeats to Heaney and Longley.

There are our entrepreneurs, including those in the State

and co-operative sectors, who created livelihoods and helped stem emigration. There are those who cared for others, in sickness and in old age. There are those who laboured to mend communal relations on this island. Come to think of it, the heroes are all over the place.

Alternatively perhaps, we should just sing with the Punks: '*No more heroes anymore.*'

Liam Kennedy is Professor Emeritus of Economic and Social History at Queen's University Belfast. His book, *Unhappy the Land, The Most Oppressed People Ever, The Irish?* is published by Merrion Press.

Peter Thompson had stumbled across an unlikely love story by chance, and apart from being intrigued by the romance of it, and the manner in which he discovered it, I was also captivated by Peter himself. From his home in the Co. Antrim village of Dervock, he spoke of healing old wounds between North and South, and the need to reclaim 1916 as a shared history for everybody on the island of Ireland. His inclusive take on this centenary year had me hooked. An avid historian, Peter told me he planned to travel to Dublin for the official opening of the 1916 exhibition in Collins Barracks in March, which he did. When he got there, a staff member shook his hand and welcomed him as the very first visitor, at which Peter replied to the amusement of the official, "Here's one for your history books: your very first visitor is an Ulster Protestant."

The Orangeman and the
Cumann na mBan Typist

For County Antrim man Peter Thompson, the Easter Rising provides the starting point for an extraordinary Romeo and Juliet love story that spanned Ulster's sectarian divide.

In happy contrast to Shakespeare's star-crossed lovers however, staunch Unionist and Somme veteran George McBride and Winifred Carney, a pistol-packing member of Cumann na mBan and secretary to James Connolly, went on to enjoy many years of happy marriage after the momentous events of 1916.

An avid historian from the village of Dervock, Peter discovered the unlikely tale quite by chance in 1985 while fundraising locally for a wall mural to commemorate the Battle of the Somme.

"There was £150 left over in the kitty, so we decided to donate it to a hospital for veterans in Belfast, known as the Somme Hospital, now the Somme nursing home," he recalls. "When we handed over the cash, a nurse asked if we'd like to meet one of the veterans.

"They wheeled in this gentleman called George McBride, who told us how he'd fought in the 36th (Ulster) Division in the First World War and was captured at the Somme and held as a prisoner of war. For me, this was fascinating stuff, but then when he moved on to his personal life, I could hardly believe my ears.

"On his return to Belfast in 1919, George joined the Labour Party, where he met and fell in love with Winifred Carney. Now this was no ordinary love story. George, a Protestant born in the Shankill Road in Belfast, was a member of the Ulster Volunteer Force and then joined the Ulster Division to fight for his king and country, while Winifred, a Catholic from Co. Down, was a key figure in the 1916 Rising.

"Known as the 'typist with the Webley' because of the revolver she carried along with her typewriter as James Connolly's secretary, she never left Connolly's side throughout the fighting in the GPO. She and her Cumann na mBan colleagues were subsequently interned in Kilmainham Jail and later Aylesbury Prison in England, until December 1916."

In 1924 she too joined the Northern Ireland Labour Party and was struck by Cupid's arrow when the handsome Orangeman won her heart. The pair were married in 1928.

"They had much in common in that both fought for their country, and were captured and imprisoned, but at the end of the day, he was a staunch Ulster Unionist and she was an equally patriotic Irish Nationalist," says Peter. "How two political idealists on completely different sides could marry was unheard of! I asked George how they dealt with that and he just said, 'We left that side of things alone.' I was mesmerised."

The marriage was not accepted by some of their friends and there's no doubt the couple would have been ostracised in many social circles, but, as Peter says, "George and Winnie were in love and that's all that mattered – that and their shared belief in socialism."

They lived happily in Belfast for fifteen years, and George never remarried after Winnie's death in 1943. However, while she was buried in Milltown cemetery, her beloved husband was buried elsewhere – and for years, Winnie's grave remained unmarked.

On the wildgeese website, Winnie's great niece Joan Austin explains: "Uncle Ernest refused to put a headstone on Aunt Winnie's grave due to her marriage to Orangeman and protestant, George McBride. The National Graves Association stepped in and recognised Winnie by erecting her well-deserved headstone, while tending her grave to this day."

Amid all the sectarianism that Northern Ireland has gone through, this unlikely love story is seen by some as a beacon of hope that shone decades before the peace process started healing old wounds between North and South.

"We have a shared history, and I think our past should bring people on the island of Ireland together, not keep us apart," says Peter. "Some people try to force history into today's politics and there's no need."

Peter is actively involved in historical events both in his own village and in cross-community projects throughout Ireland. Reconciliation through cultural understanding and respect is part of his ethos.

"I joined re-enactments of the 1798 rebellion – some say the forerunner to the 1916 Rising – in Mayo and Wexford, and made some great friends there," he says. "And in turn, when these people came to my village of Dervock as part of a local Council cross-community project, I gave them a tour and told them stories about the place and they loved it.

"I told them how, in 1835, Lord George McCartney, who owned Dervock at the time, put a toll on horses coming into the village. One workman called Nevin refused to pay, and he recruited Daniel O'Connell to represent him in court. O'Connell won the case and thereafter the horse became known throughout the village as 'Custom Free.'

"I love history, regardless of where it's from, and this year of course marks the centenary of one of the momentous events in our shared past. I don't believe the events of 1916 caused the divide in this country; the barriers were already there.

"My great grandfather, William John Cheatley, was a Lance Corporal in the 2nd Battalion Irish Rifles, stationed at Portobello Barracks, during the Easter Rising. I want to visit

Dublin this year and see the sights for myself, to go where he was and stand in the ground where he stood.

"The Easter Rising is part of the tapestry of our shared culture and history. I know that many Unionists disown it, arguing it has nothing to do with us, but it has. 1916 is part of who we are, all of us. If we don't study this important part of our history, understand it and learn from it, we damn future generations to come."

Actor, screenwriter, activist and Traveller, John Connors has a fire in him that both rages and shines a beautiful bright light. His great grandfather Patrick Ward risked his life for his country in 1916, and as far as John is concerned, that country has consistently failed his people ever since. He laid bare the anger at what he calls the 'last accepted form of racism' meted out to Travellers in Ireland today, and spoke of their rich cultural heritage in which he takes enormous pride. It was a hugely satisfying interview and, a few months later, when he was promoting a TV documentary called 'I Am Traveller,' I got to explore these issues with him further. I see John as one of the great activists of our time, one who is unlikely to ever give up fighting for equal rights and equal opportunities for Travellers. And reader, he's only in his twenties. Imagine all he has still to offer.

'My Great Grandfather, the Warrior'

Best known as bomb-maker Patrick who gunned down drug kingpin Nidge in the gritty crime drama *Love/Hate*, in real life, actor John Connors is a rebel with a cause of a different kind.

Describing discrimination against Travellers as "the last acceptable form of racism," he says nothing has changed for his people in the last hundred years when Irish Volunteers, including his great grandfather, Patrick Ward, put their lives on the line for their country. Patrick, from Tuam, Co. Galway, was only sixteen when he joined the garrison at Roe's Distillery in Dublin during the Easter Rising.

"He and his uncle and cousin were among those who fought for the promise of a socialist republic where all people would be treated equally, as set out in the Proclamation," says

John. "And look at us now, Travellers living in Third World conditions in a First World country, on sites without electricity, families evicted and told to put their children into care… Where's the equality in that?"

John's inspiration comes from his great grandfather, whose story aroused in him a passion for history and social justice.

"Patrick was fearless. At fourteen, when his father and older brother went to fight in the First World War, he got a fake birth certificate and went to Coventry to join them, but his father sent him home. A few months later, his father and brother were killed in action.

"After the Rising, Patrick was jailed along with the other rebels, and he served a further eighteen months in prison after fighting against the Treaty in the War of Independence. I'd heard a bit about him growing up, but when I saw a picture of him on the wall of a Travellers' centre in Balbriggan, I asked my grandfather to tell me more.

"I started doing some research of my own online and as I got to know more about Patrick Ward, I couldn't have been more proud. He had warrior blood in his veins. He had a profound effect on me."

After his imprisonment, Patrick went back on the road. He married a half-settled, half-Traveller woman called Bridget and they had ten children, two of whom died as babies. But Patrick came to a tragic end when, in 1942, while camping in Athlone, the local landowner, Joseph Lee, accused him of rabbit-snaring.

"This was later proved to be untrue," says John.

"Somebody else was found to have been snaring rabbits on the estate, but Lee ordered him to leave. They argued – Patrick protested he needed time – but Lee was having none of it. He shot him dead.

"In his statement Lee said, 'I killed a tinker today. I lost the head. I killed him.' Later he retracted that statement and said it was an accident. He got six months for killing my great grandfather. Six months! After everything Patrick had done for his country."

Bridget went back to Dublin and raised her family in Summerhill in the city centre. Some of her children stayed and some went back on the road, including John's grandfather, Paddy. John himself was born in London and a year later his parents returned to Ireland.

"We lived in camps, mostly in the Coolock area of Dublin, where I live today. I came back here recently after six years of living in a house. I like having extended family around and being surrounded by people I trust.

"In my line of work, you get noticed by the public and that attention can turn some people into hot air balloons. It feeds the ego. Travellers wouldn't let you away with any nonsense. We're grounded, because we know who we are and we're proud of it."

Acting is not a common career path in the Travelling community, but John hopes his own success will pave the way for other young Travellers to tread the boards.

"Travellers are the best storytellers in the world, and acting is a form of storytelling too, so I'm not surprised that I was drawn to it."

Straight out of the Gaiety acting school, John landed the lead role in the film *King of the Travellers*, then along came the gritty and hugely popular series *Love/Hate*, and this year the 26-year-old has yet more exciting projects in the pipeline, including an RTE documentary which he will present in March, about the often strained relationships between Travellers and the settled community. He's also turned his hand to screenwriting and his film, *Cardboard Gangsters* premieres this summer.

"It's about young lads who start out as low-level drug dealers. I play the lead role, Jay, who falls on hard times when his girlfriend becomes pregnant and his mother's house is taken away. He starts dealing heroin, and comes into conflict with the local kingpin. It's a gangster movie that's rooted in social realism.

"My great grandfather made me politically aware and that informs a lot of what I do. I'm massively inspired by him."

That inspiration extends to using his celebrity to train the spotlight on the cause of the travelling community.

"Travellers are an ethnic minority and we want to be recognised as such, here in our country of origin. We have a cultural tradition of our own and a shared history that distinguishes us from other groups, yet successive Irish governments deny what the UK, USA and other countries recognise as a distinct ethnic group.

"They try to assimilate us into the settled community and destroy our culture, but we won't be broken.

"The promise of a just and equal society that Patrick and his comrades fought for in 1916 has not yet been realised, but I haven't given up hope."

How do you turn a kernel of an idea into what Irish Independent reviewer Pat Stacey described as "a big, lavishly produced slab of prestige television"? It takes time and money, of course, but it also needs somebody with vision to push it forward. In the case of RTE's documentary series '1916,' narrated by Liam Neeson and hailed by critics as one of the triumphs of the broadcasting year, it took six years, almost three million euro and someone with passion and dedication to bring it from concept to conclusion. That someone was Irish academic at the University of Notre Dame, Bríona NicDhiarmada. Her enthusiasm was infectious as she told me why she felt it was important to put the Easter Rising in a global context, how she'd been inspired by acclaimed American documentary maker Ken Burns, and how she managed to bring together the right team at the right time to make the magic happen.

Six Days that Shook
the World

For such a pivotal episode in modern Irish history, it's easy to lose sight of the fact that the 1916 Easter Rising also had a major impact on world history, the reverberations of which could be felt long after the guns had fallen silent in Dublin's shattered city centre.

According to the producer and writer of *1916*, a new three-part documentary, the doomed rebellion was likewise subject to influences from far beyond Ireland's shores at a time when seismic events were beginning to undermine the established global order.

The brainchild of Professor Bríona Nic Dhiarmada, a fellow of the Keough-Naughton Institute for Irish Studies and Chair of Irish Language and Literature at the University of

Notre Dame, the documentary casts new light on this iconic 100-year-old story by placing it within the context of what was happening in the wider world at that time.

She says the inspiration for the documentary came from Ken Burns's highly acclaimed series about the American Civil War.

"I wanted to put the Easter Rising in its international context, and try and do for Irish history what Ken Burns achieved in his excellent documentary," she says. "The Rising coincided with the rise of socialism, women's suffrage and revolutionary fervour that swept across Europe, not to mention the centrality of Irish-America which had a huge bearing on events here.

"The number of people who died during the Rising paled into insignificance compared with those killed in the Somme. Yet, from the archives of the *New York Times*, we discovered the Rising made front page headlines in the NY Times for fourteen consecutive days, pushing stories about WW1 into second place. And they weren't sympathetic, at least not in the early days, but after the executions, 20,000 people lined the streets of New York in protest.

"At the same time, India was also looking to Ireland, as it identified with the idea of self-determination and rising up against a common enemy. But while Ghandi and Nehru didn't like the Sinn Féin example, the radical Subhal Chandra Bose in Bengal was directly influenced by the Irish experience. On Good Friday 1930, a group of revolutionaries known as the

Indian Republican Army took over the post office in Chittagong (now in Bangladesh) and staged their own Easter Rising. The leaders were later arrested and hanged.

"Other nations under British rule reasoned if this little country could stand up to Britain, then so could they. During a rally for independence in British East Africa (now Tanzania), civilians held a banner which read, '*Africa will be free, by Hook or by Crook.*' This was significant, because that phrase originated in Oliver Cromwell's famous claim, 'I will take Ireland by Hook or by Crook,' referring to Hook Head in Co. Wexford and Crook, Co. Waterford."

Narrated by Liam Neeson, the series combines archive footage, photos and drawings with contributions from Irish and international historians who show the Rising in the context of the time in which it was set.

"It's easy to be cynical of the Proclamation of Independence in the light of today, but Ireland was not a liberal democracy when it was drawn up," says Bríona. "Only sixty percent of people could vote. No woman could vote. People had difficult choices to make.

"History is far from black and white, it's full of nuance, so demonising the Rising leaders as a bunch of lunatics serves as little purpose as making them holier-than-thou heroes. It's the complications and contradictions of it all that I find most interesting.

"We've put back parts of history that were taken out, whether through accident or design. This is as much a part of

British history as it is Irish. The British soldiers were so young and inexperienced, many who arrived in Kingstown, now Dun Laoghaire, thought they were in France. Most had never fired a gun before and within hours, hundreds were dead.

"I hope the series goes some way to restore a little pride in ourselves as a nation. We do far too much self-flagellation, and we have much to be proud of. For instance, the Irish army is one of the few never to have gone to war in the last century, we've been peacekeepers and exemplars for other countries who have not been a colonial power. For our size, we've had a ripple effect across the world."

Costing close to €3 million to make, the documentary was largely funded by the University of Notre Dame and its sponsors, with twenty percent of the budget coming from RTE and Section 481 funding. The three-part series was aired on TV, while a seventy-minute cinematic version was shown in the National Concert Hall on March 16th and simulcasted in Irish embassies to local audiences worldwide.

"Chris Fox, Director of the Keough-Naughton Institute for Irish Studies at Notre Dame and I worked hand in glove," says Bríona. "We were very fortunate that Liam Neeson came on board at an early stage, we had researchers digging into archives worldwide, and all the shooting and pre- and post-production were done in Ireland.

"Together with my co-producer Jackie Larkin, we were able to put together a really experienced, creative team, including Ruán Magan who co-wrote the script, designer Anne

Atkins who won an Oscar for best production design for the film *The Grand Budapest Hotel*, and Linda Cullen and Stuart Switzer of Irish production company, CoCo Television.

"When we took it to a distributor for public service broadcasting in the United States, it was immediately taken up by a hundred and twenty stations coast to coast. Now that really is phenomenal."

1916 is available on DVD from usual outlets. A companion book to the series, *The 1916 Irish Rebellion*, is published by Cork University Press.

One hundred years ago, Irish people rose up and fought for their country; now they rise up and leave their country. Author Kevin Curran is part of a generation for whom the emigration trail appeared the only path on offer when the Celtic Tiger bubble burst. In his novel, Citizens, he bridges the gap between 1916 and the present, and it's not always a pretty picture. It charts the story of Neil, whose grandfather dies, leaving memoirs that describe a newsreel he filmed during the Easter Rising. At first Neil wonders if the newsreel can be found, whether its sale might pay for his flight to Canada. As he reads on, however, he discovers the real value of his grandfather's legacy and what it means to be Irish. In real life, Kevin is the great grandson of Harry Colley, a Fianna Fáil TD whose son George Colley held a number of Cabinet posts. Kevin was not tempted to follow their footsteps into politics.

'I'm Filling in the
Gaps of 1916'

Holy Thursday 1916: Harry Colley – later to become father of Fianna Fail politician George Colley – parades with F Company, 2nd Battalion Auxilliary Volunteers in Dublin's Father Matthew Park. Thomas MacDonagh addresses the gathering.

Sunday's manoevres will be most important, he tells them. If any man is not prepared to fight, now is the time to get out; no one will think any the worse of him. Those who choose to fight needn't worry about their dependents; they have friends in America who'll take care of them.

"It was clear the hour had come," Harry recalled in his witness statement in 1966.

Despite the confusion that followed Eoin MacNeill's

famous countermanding order three days later, Harry, then twenty-five, and his fellow volunteers remobilised on Easter Monday, after his mother had embraced him and said, 'Go and do your duty to your country.'

And so he did, not only during the Easter Rising, but for decades later as a leading figure in Irish politics.

A century later, his great grandson, Kevin Curran, has drawn on Harry's experiences in *Citizens*, a novel that starkly contrasts the idealism of 1916's revolutionaries with the disenchantment of 21st Century youth, marred by unemployment and emigration.

One hundred years ago people rose and fought for their country, he remarks; now they rise and leave their country, many never to return.

"The sad reality is that many of the people for whom I wrote this book are no longer here," says Kevin. "There are 205,000 fewer twenty-somethings in Ireland now than six years ago. They might have feelings for their homeland, but the tragedy is they were forced to emigrate.

"What use is nationalism when you have to leave? We need a relationship with the past, but what does this centenary mean to today's wave of emigrants who've been eased out of the narrative?

"I'm thirty-four and a lot of my friends are now in Canada, Australia, the United States and elsewhere. My brother is four years younger and his circle of college friends is decimated. They're all gone."

Kevin considers himself one of the lucky ones. An English teacher in Balbriggan, Co. Dublin, he's married with two children, Sebastian and Fleur, and still finds time to write. He's been working on *Citizens*, his second novel, since 2012.

"I used my great grandfather's letters, but as a plot device, I put a Pathé newsreel in the hands of my protagonist, Harry Casey. I wanted to find a way to bridge the gap between his past and the contemporary world. The moving image is how we exist today. We talk to each other through devices, and in 1916, the newsreel was the new technology."

Throughout the story, Casey mirrors Harry Colley's real-life movements from Easter Monday to the following Thursday, when Harry almost died.

Shot in the ankle as he beat a retreat from the old Imperial Hotel, above Clery's department store, he saw a barricade ahead. He fixed his bayonet and lunged at a British soldier, but in jumping over the barricade, the soldier lunged back at him, stabbed him in the thigh and punctured his lung.

Suppressing the urge to cry out in pain, Harry said, "I was not going to let these British soldiers hear me moaning.'

A soldier grabbed him by the collar and laid him on top of their barricade as extra cover, and shot over him. A few minutes later he was pushed to the ground.

"I thought my neck was broken," said Harry.

He fell unconscious and woke in the Castle Hospital, where he drifted in and out of consciousness, hearing voices now and then like that of a priest giving him the last rites, and a doctor saying, 'Serves him right, mixing with that lot.'

Six weeks later he was interned in Kilmainham Jail and from there sent by boat to Frongoch Prison in Wales.

On arrival at Holyhead, the prisoners sang rebel songs, and when an English officer warned them to be quiet or he'd open fire, they defiantly raised their voices even louder to the strains of *The Soldier's Song*.

After the Rising Harry helped found Fianna Fail in 1926 and held a Dáil seat for fourteen years until finally defeated by the young Charles Haughey. He later became a Senator.

Harry's son George followed him into politics and held every office apart from Taoiseach. It was George who coined the phrase, 'Low standards in high places,' in reference to the Haughey era. (Haughey defeated George Colley in the 1979 party leadership election by just a handful of votes).

"We're all proud of Harry and George, but while I have an interest in politics, I'm not affiliated with any party," says Kevin. "I just wanted to tell Harry's story, but while the military history records are fascinating, the language is a bit stiff. I set out to fill in what was left unspoken.

"We know the history of the Rising, but to try and get into the shoes of those involved, to feel what they felt, I think that can only be created in novel form."

The result is a thumping good yarn that weaves actual historical events with a personal story of passion, patriotism and betrayal. It's told through the eyes of a 26-year-old unemployed Dubliner who's planning to emigrate to Canada once he gets what's bequeathed to him by his late grandfather, and what a legacy it turns out to be.

Citizens by Kevin Curran is published by Liberties Press.

*Colonel George Arthur French, the British army officer charged
with putting an end to the Rising in Enniscorthy, Co. Wexford, is
remembered for doing so with humanity, courtesy and respect. I
had the great pleasure of speaking for almost an hour on the phone
with his grandson, Arthur French, from his home in New Forest,
England, and if our chat was anything to go by, I can easily
imagine what a deft negotiator his grandfather must have been.
Not only was Arthur proud of what his grandfather had
accomplished in achieving surrender without bloodshed, he was
excited about the upcoming commemorations. He planned to travel
to Wexford where he said, "I am much looking forward to events
in Enniscorthy over Easter weekend." He made the trip and
delighted in all the spectacle of the celebrations. Sadly, Arthur died
on June 17th 2016. R.I.P. to an officer and a gentleman.*

An Officer and a
Gentleman

With its thousands of casualties and city centre devastation, Easter week 1916 in Dublin underlines the brutal truth that most conflicts are remembered in direct proportion to the scale of human suffering they entail.

In that light, events in the capital overshadowed the simultaneous rising in Enniscorthy, Co Wexford that concluded in a far less bloody manner. That it did not end in carnage was in large part due to the humane actions of a local farmer and retired British army colonel who found himself recalled to service in response to the Rising.

Famously immortalised as a key site of the 1798 rebellion, County Wexford rose again in Easter week when local units of the Irish Volunteers took control of Enniscorthy. It was in these potentially explosive circumstances that retired Colonel George Arthur French (1864-1950) received a telegraph from the British War Office instructing him to take command of crown forces in the model county.

Looking back on the events of that fateful week, his grandson Arthur recalls that Colonel French had settled back in the family seat in Newbay after first retiring from the army in 1912; he rejoined at the outbreak of war and retired again in 1915. He was considered too old to remain on the active list in 1916, but that changed when the Enniscorthy Rising occurred.

For five days, hopes of victory had been high as 1,000 volunteers mobilised throughout the county. But as the British authorities prepared their response, the potential for heavy loss of life was very real.

Another commander might easily have razed Enniscorthy in retaliation, but Colonel French is said to have treated the rebels with courtesy. Crucially, he arranged a military escort for Captains Seamus Doyle and Sean Etchingham to visit Padraig Pearse in Arbour Hill Barracks, Dublin and return with his written order to surrender.

On May 1st 1916, Colonel French received their unconditional surrender in Enniscorthy and over the following days 375 people were arrested in Co Wexford, many of whom were subsequently detained in prisons in England and Wales.

"Possibly because he was Irish, and a Wexford man through and through, he was favourably disposed to the people in his community, and they to him," says Arthur.

It's said there were up to 2,000 Crown troops under Colonel French's command, but according to Arthur, it didn't start out that way.

"He had only a handful of cadets from the local army, no more than grown-up boys, but by the end of the week reinforcements arrived as the War Office had promised.

"More were likely on the way and George knew he had to act fast. Had some hardline English commander been in his position, I have no doubt he would have knocked the whole place flat. But my grandfather didn't want to see Enniscorthy blown sky high - he lived there; this was his own community - so he reached a gentlemen's solution with the Irish Volunteers.

"It also helped that the people conducting the Rising in Enniscorthy were well organised. If as a military officer you're dealing with a riot with no visible person in charge, negotiation is impossible. But these were people George Arthur clearly felt he could reason with. They had a chain of command and took responsibility for their actions."

Coming from a long line of military officers, it's not surprising that Arthur also made a career in the British Army. He joined the Royal Irish Fusiliers in 1954 - "I wouldn't consider any other regiment!" - and his first posting was to Kenya. The army life clearly gave him an understanding of his grandfather's actions in 1916.

"I'm enormously proud of him, because he saved bloodshed in Enniscorthy, not to mention the needless destruction of property. Above all, he was a good, honest, decent man. Neither of my grandparents' families thought of themselves as English, in spite of Colonel George Arthur's British military career, and herein lies the key to his handling of the situation.

"He organised a British Legion parade for the soldiers returning at the end of the war, many of whom had fought at the Somme. It must have been very difficult for them when they came back to a changed Ireland, in which many were not well received."

The French family's lineage dates back to the Normans who landed at Bannow Bay, Co Wexford, under the command of Robert Fitz-Stephen. Some settled in Roscommon, where the Colonel's more famous father, also called George Arthur, and a relative of songwriter Percy French, was born.

"My great grandfather was a British Army officer who became the first commissioner of the North West Mounted Police in Canada – the Mounties," says Arthur. "He rose to the rank of Major General in the British Army, and received a knighthood on his retirement in 1902.

"My grandmother's family, the Jefferies, migrated from Wexford to South America after 1798. Having done quite well for themselves in Montevideo, Uruguay, her parents returned to Wexford with a herd of cattle and bought Newbay House in 1869. Annie Elizabeth (Koten) remained in Uruguay for another twenty years before coming to Ireland. She married my grandfather George Arthur in 1899 and Newbay House passed into the French family."

Arthur spent holidays there as a child - his mother had taken her children to Scotland at the outbreak of World War II, and he went from there to school in England - but although he settled in Hampshire, he doesn't consider himself English.

"I'm neither English nor Anglo-Irish. In fact, I've got no English blood whatsoever. My mother's family was entirely from Scotland and my father's entirely from Ireland, so I'm half-Irish, half-Scots."

Arthur is enormously proud of his roots and he plans to be in Enniscorthy on Easter Monday this year to be part of the centenary commemorations.

"The Easter Rising was too early in terms of achieving independence for Ireland, so it ended up being a bit of a shambles, but it had to happen," he says. "It was simply ahead of its time."

When Rotunda Maternity Hospital archivist Anne O'Byrne was asked to curate an exhibition about this landmark institution's role in the Easter Rising, she hadn't much time to do it - six months tops. It was truly a labour of love, and no easy delivery... (Okay, I'll stop). Anne told me about the strange confluence of events that linked the cruelty of British Captain Percival Lea-Wilson towards the rebels in his charge after the Rising with the recent acquisition by the National Gallery of a priceless Caravaggio. And then there was the irony of a young midwife Mary O'Shea who, having spent two years in France during the First World War, looked forward "with great joy" to returning to Ireland "to peace, quiet and happiness." And where did she find herself in Easter Week 1916? The Rotunda, with a bird's eye view of the epic battle raging on the streets below.

Giving Birth
to a Nation

It's one of the National Gallery's best-known paintings, a priceless treasure that was lost for decades before making international headlines when it turned up in a Jesuit residence. What's far less well known is that Caravaggio's '*The Taking of Christ*' has a direct connection to 1916 in a poignant tale involving an iconic rebel leader, an assassinated RIC officer and his grieving widow.

The story begins in the immediate aftermath of Easter Week when Captain Percival Lea-Wilson became a marked man after he abused and humiliated prisoners in his charge after they were marched from the GPO to the Rotunda Hospital.

According to onlookers, one of Lea-Wilson's worst offences was to order Thomas Clarke, then fifty-nine, to be stripped naked and forced to stand on the hospital steps in view of the nurses. He also taunted Seán MacDermott, who walked with a limp caused by polio, calling him a "cripple."

Watching intently close by was a young Michael Collins, who swore that he would avenge the humiliation of his comrades.

He did so four years later when, on 15th June 1920, Lea-Wilson was shot dead outside his home in Gorey, Co. Wexford on Collins's orders. In the wake of the killing, his widow, Dr Marie Lea-Wilson turned to a Jesuit priest for solace. In return, in what she considered a fitting gesture of gratitude, she gave him a painting attributed to a Dutch artist, Gerard von Honthorst, which she had previously acquired for less than the equivalent of $1,000 in Edinburgh.

And there the story would have ended but for the fact that, after decades lost in storage, Caravaggio's masterpiece caused a sensation when it was rediscovered in 1990.

It's a sequence of events that has left connoisseurs and historians alike to ponder that if Lea-Wilson hadn't humiliated the leaders of the Rising, he wouldn't have been murdered, his widow wouldn't have sought counselling from the Jesuits, who in turn would not have received the painting – and Ireland would most likely have lost a priceless treasure.

This is one of many 1916 stories that forms part of a new exhibition, 'The Rotunda – Birth of a Nation.'

Just up the road from the rebels' GPO headquarters during Easter week, staff and patients in the world's oldest maternity hospital had a unique view of events from the vantage point of the iconic Rotunda building on Parnell Square. Among them was Mary O'Shea, a 23-year-old midwifery trainee from Abbeyleix, whose handwritten memoir of what she saw during that week will be on display at the exhibition.

Having spent the previous two years in France at the outbreak of the First World War, Mary wrote how it was "*with great joy I returned to Ireland to peace, quiet and happiness.*"

But that peace was shattered when the Rising began and she watched "in fascinated horror" as a new war unfolded before her very eyes.

"*Easter week 1916 seemed so unreal that even still it seems like a nightmare,*" she wrote, remembering how she and her colleagues tended to their patients, while on the street below, people were shot and dragged off to the Rotunda morgue, and at night "*the whole sky seemed illuminated.*"

"*Here we were, with lovely dear old Dublin falling down about us and we trying to calm people who had not a clue about what was happening.*"

Paying no heed to warnings to stay away from the windows, Mary kept a close eye on events outside.

"*We saw snipers at work from the top of the houses of Parnell Square. We saw all the prisoners collected into the lawn in front of the houses of the hospital and marched away to prison. One I think was the Countess, judging by the size of her small hands and feet.*

"*When things got quiet and we went out of doors, a terrible sight met our eyes. O'Connell Street in a shambles."*

With the GPO in ruins following the Rising, the Postmaster General set up temporary sorting offices in the 'Rotunda Rink,' a large steel and wooden structure which stood in the grounds now occupied by the Garden of Remembrance. It might have become a permanent arrangement had anti-Treaty troops not doused the building in petrol and set it alight on November 5th 1922.

By that time, Mary O'Shea had returned from England where she had done her general nursing training only to find the country in the midst of a civil war that she described as "a thousand times worse" than what had gone on in 1916.

"To think that lads who stood together against a common foe could split and be so bitter," she wrote. *"This to me is the tragedy of our time."*

Mary is one of five women of the Rising celebrated in the Rotunda exhibition, which also features Bridget Lyons Thornton, Kathleen Lynn, Dorothy Stopford Price and the Honourable Albinia Broderick. For the Rotunda's Head Librarian Anne O'Byrne, the project was a labour of love, but with only six months from conception, it was no easy delivery.

"It was very much a collaborative effort involving doctors, nurses, heads of departments, partners like the Abbeyleix Heritage Company and our special adviser, historian Sinead McCoole," she says. "We were delighted to contribute to the centenary commemorations."

The exhibition also showed that it was not only the Easter

Rising that claimed lives in 1916. The squalid conditions in Dublin's overcrowded tenements led to mothers and babies frequently dying from vomiting bugs and other diseases, conditions which are easily treated today.

Forget about the notion of the artist struggling in a garret, cut off from social discourse. Michael Fortune and Aileen Lambert have so many creative projects on the go at any one time, it's hard to keep up. When it came to 1916, they set out to preserve the stories, songs, poetry and folklore of the era, involving their community every step of the way - literally. One of their ventures, 'Backroads to the Rising,' involved people retracing the steps of their forebears in a march from towns and villages throughout the county to Enniscorthy on Easter Monday. It was a perfect example of how local communities took ownership of their own commemoration activities this year and expressed themselves in imaginative ways. Mind you, Michael is also concerned that a century after a rebellion that was as much cultural as political, today's generation appears to have something of an identity crisis.

'We Need to Restore
Confidence in Our Nation'

For decades after the bloody rebellion of 1798, families across Wexford kept alive the immortal warning of their forefathers to "keep the pike in the thatch."

The message was clear: locals were urged to conceal their weapons in the roofs of their homes in readiness for another Rising. The caution passed into folklore down through generations and 118 years later was literally heeded as rebels from the model county once again armed themselves with pikes.

By 1916, the use of such primitive weapons was a necessity borne out of a lack of modern rifles, yet in spite of this crucial disadvantage, local volunteers played a significant part in the events of Easter Week 1916, with Wexford becoming the scene of the biggest Rising outside the capital and the last place where rebels surrendered.

This is one of many anecdotes that appear in *1916 Stories*, a collection of personal tales of the Rising produced by local artists and historians Michael Fortune and his partner Aileen Lambert from Ballindaggin.

"It's important to highlight these details, because while stories about 1798 and the famine survived locally, there's a lot we don't know about 1916 and the years that followed," says Michael. "Families were so devastated by the Civil War they refused to speak of it, and it became a terrible secret that blighted generations.

"At my own grandmother's wake last year, a man showed me a picture of her first cousin, a prominent figure in the Irish Republican Army, who took the anti-Treaty side in the war. I'd never seen it before, or heard of his activities. Was she ashamed? I'll never know, because she never talked about it. Certain things were simply not spoken about."

And while this year's centenary provides the perfect opportunity to lift that cloak of silence, Michael suspects the rebels of 1916 might spin in their sacrificial graves if they could hear the chatter of today's generation.

"1916 was as much a cultural revolution as a political one and I wonder what those involved would think of the homogenised, hybrid, faux-American/English accent that trips off the tongues of our young generation. Even our national broadcasters are at it. It's not confined to Dublin's middle classes; it's everywhere. To me, this demonstrates a widespread lack of confidence in ourselves as a nation.

"Language and accents change gradually, over time, but in the last twenty years, a dramatic shift to this new hybrid accent and its accompanying affectations has spread throughout the country.

"Since the late 1990s, the term, 'the UK' has slipped into our vocabulary and, I believe, whitewashes the cultural identities of our Welsh, Scottish and English neighbours. Are we aware as Irish people what this means, historically and globally?

"If there's one thing we could all do to mark the centenary of 1916, it's to reflect on who we are and where we have come from. Without a sense of who we are locally, we will slowly gravitate to a homogenised, global cultural identity, controlled by god knows whom, where we are told how to sound, eat, dress and think.

"It's ironic that regional accents throughout England are prized by many, while in Ireland we have a generation of people putting on fake so-called posh English accents in order to cover up their particular Irish one. If it wasn't so serious, it'd be funny."

Other activities close to Michael's heart are his and Aileen's traditional music and song projects, *The 1916 Song Project*, and *Children of the Revolution*, and a walking/cycling event called *Backroads to the Rising*. From 7am on Easter Monday, people will retrace the steps of the men and women who walked and cycled from various towns and villages to raise the national flag over Enniscorthy, which this year will stage one of the biggest parades outside Dublin.

Michael and Aileen's 1916 projects form part of the Wexford centenary commemorations programme co-ordinated by District Manager Padraig O'Gorman, who says it's been a decade in the planning.

"For the past fifty years we've held a 1916 commemoration every Easter Monday, so it's already part of our tradition. Ten years ago, Wexford County Council started putting a small budget aside each year towards the centenary. Then, eighteen months ago, we set up a dedicated committee and asked local people how they wanted 1916 to be commemorated.

"The answers were clear: they wanted something dignified, reflective, solemn and inspiring, but most of all, there should be a legacy for the youth of the county. We put together an information pack for primary and secondary schools so children could connect with this part of their history, and it's been very well received."

Another key member of the committee is Wexford County Council archivist Grainne Doran, who's given lectures, written articles and curated exhibitions in Enniscorthy Castle and the Athenaeum, the building Volunteers made their headquarters during the Rising. Among her many projects are a Day of Letters in the town library, a Cumann na mBan tea party, the publication of a previously unseen diary account of the Rising by Goddard Orpen, a member of the local gentry, and a presentation of certificates to the relatives of those who took part in the Rising.

"The Easter Rising is part of the tapestry of the culture and history of Wexford," she says. "It means a lot to the people of our county that we commemorate the brave men and women of 1916 for their extraordinary determination, perseverance and zeal in furthering the cause for national independence."

Diocesan archivist Noelle Dowling gave me a fascinating glimpse into the lives of priests who ministered to the wounded, heard confessions and anointed the dead in the war zone that was Dublin in 1916. She was deeply moved by many of the accounts she read, including that of Fr Eugene McCarthy, who witnessed James Connolly's execution. He reported that Connolly slumped so badly when tied to a chair that soldiers instead strapped him to a stretcher which they reclined against a wall, presumably to get a better shot. Fr Francis Farrington, the priest brought to Arbour Hill on May 3rd to preside over the funerals of the executed leaders, said their remains arrived "in pools of blood, still warm and limp, eyes bandaged and mouths open." Such was the horror of the executions for both the victims and those who witnessed them.

Brothers in Arms:
The Priests of 1916

Amid the crossfire and inferno on the streets of Dublin during the 1916 Rising, priests throughout the city found themselves thrown into a role for which few were prepared - that of providing comfort in battle.

Based in Church Street, the Capuchins were caught up in the action, and while civilians took refuge in the Pro Cathedral across from the GPO, priests there came and went, dodging bullets to tend to the wounded and dying. It was a mission few had ever expected to experience, but according to Dublin diocesan archivist Noelle Dowling, they rose to the challenge even at great personal cost.

The most senior figure in the church at the time, Archbishop William Walsh, relied heavily on his secretary,

Monsignor Michael Curran, to keep him informed on what was happening on the ground.

"Archbishop Walsh was very ill in 1916," says Noelle. "He'd developed a severe attack of eczema which lasted over a year. On Good Friday, April 21st 1916, he was bandaged from head to toe and his illness was at its height.

"For somebody who was so active – he used to cycle regularly to Maynooth and back – being housebound must have been very difficult."

Monsignor Curran was his eyes and ears, from Easter Monday when he cycled into town and met Padraig Pearse whom he described as 'flushed, but calm and authoritative' and asked if there was anything he could do. Pearse replied, 'No, we're going to see it out.'

However, some Volunteers wanted to go to confession, he said, so the Monsignor arranged this with the priests from the Pro Cathedral. By two o'clock that afternoon, he noted that looting had begun, started by women and children helping themselves to the contents of Noblett's sweetshop.

On Thursday 27th the Archbishop's house in Drumcondra came under fire. Monsignor Curran arranged for the Archbishop to sleep on the north side of the house and barricaded the windows with mattresses. The priest secretaries slept on the ground floor corridor.

The following day, Fr Patrick Kennedy, a curate in Halston Street, was shot in the hand as he celebrated Mass when a stray bullet smashed through a stained glass window of St Michan's

Church. Fr Kennedy continued with the service as if nothing had happened.

On Saturday, when word of the Volunteers' unconditional surrender came out, the Archbishop decreed that there was no obligation to say Mass the following day, and no bells were to be rung.

"Archbishop Walsh was known for his nationalist sympathies," says Noelle. "He didn't allow World War One recruitment posters to be placed on the railings of church property and he stopped war hospital and Red Cross collections as he believed these were being used for recruitment by the government."

But while he didn't condemn the Rising as other clerical figures did in the months that followed Easter Week 1916, neither did he publicly support it.

"He worked quietly in the background and had to be very careful about what he said in exchanges with senior British government figures."

One of those was General Sir John Grenfell Maxwell, who arrived in Dublin on April 28th on the orders of Lord Kitchener, Minister for War, to quell the rising and pacify the Irish people. Prime Minister Herbert Asquith left Maxwell to his own devices in ordering the executions of the Rising leaders and, despite the Archbishop's pleas to reprieve them, the executions began at Kilmainham Jail on May 3rd.

"The priests anointed the men where they fell. Fr Eugene McCarthy, chaplain of Kilmainham Jail, did so with Joseph

Plunkett, just hours after he'd performed his marriage ceremony with Grace Gifford.

"He was also deeply troubled by James Connolly's execution. He described Connolly trying to stand like the others, but he was so badly wounded, he was unable to do so. Soldiers tied him to a chair, but he slumped so badly he overbalanced. Finally, he was strapped to a stretcher and placed in a reclining position against the wall and shot. According to his own records, the sight left an indelible mark on Fr McCarthy."

On May 3rd Fr Francis Farrington, chaplain to Arbour Hill, was collected by the military and taken to Arbour Hill to preside over the funerals of the first men to be killed – Padraig Pearse, Tomas McDonagh and Tom Clarke.

"He described hearing the volley of shots at Kilmainham and the arrival of the remains in pools of blood, still warm and limp, eyes bandaged and mouths open," says Noelle. "That's such a powerful image, it brings home to me the horror of these executions. It stops you in your tracks.

"Fr Farrington read the burial service at 4.00am and they were buried, uncoffined, in a trench sixty feet long."

Meanwhile, Maxwell sought the Archbishop's help in deporting some priests he accused of participating in the Rising. The Archbishop said he had no jurisdiction in the matter as no Dublin priests were on the list, and advised the General to contact their bishops directly. Noting that two were from Limerick gave the Archbishop a 'malicious pleasure,' according to his secretary, because he anticipated the robust response that followed when Maxwell wrote to Bishop O'Dwyer of Limerick requesting that two of his priests, Fr Tom Wall and Fr Michael Hayes, be prevented from interacting with people.

"Not only did Bishop O'Dwyer refuse his request, he wrote to him to express his horror at what he considered Maxwell's '*wantonly cruel and oppressive*' conduct in having young men shot in cold blood," says Noelle. "He said he regarded his actions with horror and believed he had outraged the conscience of the country.

"He concluded, '*Your regime has been one of the worst and blackest chapters in the history of the misgovernment of the country.*'

"The letter appeared in newspapers at home and abroad. Bishop O'Dwyer had put his head above the parapet and I believe it gave Archbishop Walsh great pleasure indeed."

I decided to make like a tourist and jumped on a mini bus doing a 1916 tour. It was a day of pure edutainment, as tour guide John Ducie explained the background to the Rising. He took us from the 1798 rebellion to the Famine, Penal Laws, Land League and other parts of history that had flown over my head at school, but now were brought to life by a man whose soft-spoken manner belied his encyclopaedic knowledge. It's hard to beat the experience of standing in the very spot where the rebels once stood, or seeing the detail of a building you might have passed your whole life without realising its significance. In Dun Laoghaire we could almost hear the apprehensive whispers of young Sherwood Foresters as they assembled in Kingstown port, seasick and disoriented, some thinking they were in France, before hundreds marched off to be shot down at Mount Street Bridge.

A Magical History Tour
of 1916

It's one of the great 'what ifs' of 1916. On the first day of the
Rising on Easter Monday, Dublin Castle was all but deserted
when a force of ten men and nine women from the Irish Citizen
Army arrived with orders to seize the nerve centre of British
power in Ireland.

Leading them was Sean Connolly, who confronted the RIC
officer on duty at the gates, demanding to be let in. But
Constable James O'Brien refused. Connolly shot him dead, one
Irish man slaying another. The Easter Rising had claimed its
first casualty.

Yet having achieved the element of surprise, Connolly
failed to press his advantage. Had he but known it, the Castle
was virtually empty. Apart from six caretakers, most of its usual

occupants had taken a day off for the bank holiday, many of them at Fairyhouse racecourse, where the Grand National attracted crowds of holidaymakers oblivious to the mayhem that was about to erupt in the city.

"It could have been a very different outcome had Connolly realised the castle was almost empty," says tour guide John Ducie. "Had his force penetrated the main gates, they could have quite easily taken the building, which would have given the rebels an important strategic advantage."

Having failed in their mission, the rebels instead occupied City Hall next door. As British reinforcements converged on the building, Connolly's force soon discovered their position was hopeless.

"City Hall was impossible to defend," John explains. "Troops on the roof of the castle started firing at the rebels on the roof of City Hall and by 2.00pm, Sean Connolly was dead."

John's speculation on how the assault on the Castle might have turned out is just one of the countless Rising stories he delivers daily on the 1916 Revolution Day Tour of Dublin. Reading about the Rising is one thing, but as the small group of Irish, Italian and Scottish people taking part in today's tour soon discover, learning about key events of the rebellion where they actually happened brings a whole new dimension to the story.

Case in point - before leaving the grounds of Dublin Castle, John points to the statue of Lady Justice atop the main gate.

"In other countries, this sculpture is typically depicted

wearing a blindfold, representing the ideal of justice being blind to discrimination," he says. "It's also usually positioned looking out over the people of the city.

"However, Dublin's iconic statue features certain characteristics that betray the kind of justice favoured by the British authorities who erected it in 1751. Her eyes are unbound, the scales slightly tilted towards the Revenue office, and she faces into the castle, hence the Dublin saying:

"The Statue of Justice, mark well her station,
Her face to the castle and arse to the nation."

Back on the bus, John sheds light on 1916 activities as we drive past the Mendicity Institution, Four Courts, the Royal Barracks and, not least, Kilmainham Jail. Then it's on to Rathfarnham and a tour of St Enda's, which Pearse set up as an example of how he felt a school should be run.

Students there were inculcated with a love of books, culture, sport, Irish language and unyielding patriotism, while a mock fort in the grounds provided an ideal venue for the boys of Na Fianna Éireann, the rebels' youth wing, to train in military exercises.

Following lunch, the tour continues to Dun Laoghaire, or Kingstown as it was known then, where British troops arrived on Wednesday April 26th 1916.

"The Sherwood Foresters, or 'Robin Hoods,' as they were known, were made up of raw young recruits, most of whom had never fired a rifle before," says John. "They assembled on the quays and received instruction in musketry, their only preparation for the disaster that was to befall them later at the Battle of Mount Street Bridge."

It was on Mount Street that a strategically placed group of only fifteen rebels held the outpost, resulting in the deaths of four officers and twenty-four other ranks of the Sherwood Foresters, and over two hundred others badly wounded.

Their Captain Frederick Dietrichsen, a 33-year-old London barrister who had married a woman from Blackrock, Co. Dublin, was surprised to run into her at the RDS as his column marched through Ballsbridge. Having warmly embraced his wife and their two children, he walked five hundred yards down the road and was shot dead.

Civilians were also killed in the massacre on Mount Street.

"Responding to the cries of the wounded, a 29-year-old dentist called Charles Hachette Hyland and his neighbour dragged injured soldiers and passers-by to his house at Percy Place and treated them there," says John.

"He paid dearly for his humanity when that night, he was killed by a passing sniper, as was the Captain of the St John's Ambulance. Such were the horrors of war for ordinary people who happened to be caught up in it."

As a "reward" for their bravery on Mount Street, the Sherwood Foresters were chosen to form the twelve-member firing squad for the executions of the Rising leaders at Kilmainham Jail.

The cold-blooded procedure had the soldiers take up position ten paces from their target, six kneeling and six standing, and on the order of the commanding officer, they would fire eleven bullets at the heart of the man before them. If necessary, the commanding officer would follow up with a single gunshot to the back of the head from a revolver.

The 1916 Revolution Day Tour of Dublin was run by Hilltop Treks.

Easter Sunday 2016 dawned at last and wild horses wouldn't have kept me from spending at least some of it in Dublin. I didn't get a press pass for any of the official events, but so what? I just wanted to be there, to feel the atmosphere, witness a parade that promised to be like no other, and be part of something big and uniquely Irish. And what a day it turned out to be. Despite fears of security threats, riots, inclement weather, acts of god or any other calamity that could possibly befall, in fact nothing rained on our parade. It was a glorious, resounding success - a joyful, proud and dignified celebration attended by hundreds of thousands of people who lined the streets of the capital. I wouldn't have missed it for the world, and the icing on the cake? When the editor called and asked if I'd write about it for the next day's Irish Independent....

This Parade Was for Us - the People of Ireland -
And We Loved It!

It was a once-in-a-lifetime event, one of those days which, like JFK's assassination and Pope John Paul's visit to Ireland, years from now will form part of a 'Where were you when...' dialogue.

This Easter parade marked something extra special, our Independence Day, and people flocked to the capital to be part of something bigger than anything we've witnessed before or likely ever will again.

It wasn't just to watch the parade up close – in such a vast sea of people, most of us were never going to get a bird's eye view – but it didn't matter. If you wanted to follow the performance, you'd have been best advised to stay at home and watch the telly. But if you wanted to know how a small country celebrates one hundred years of independence, or what it's like to experience the stirring spectacle of the Air Corps flying at 750 feet over O'Connell Street in tight wing-to-wing formation shooting out a thundering jet stream tricolour in their wake, Dublin was the only place to be.

It was the ultimate family day out. The DART in from Bray was thronged with parents and kids dressed in their Easter Sunday best. One family had come from Carrickfergus to be there. "Aye, wouldn't miss it for the world," said the dad, happily handing over a tenner to a street hawker for a pair of national flags for each of his daughters to wave - a bit pricey, but to be fair, many hawkers embraced the sprit of the day, giving added value by dressing up in the uniforms of Irish Volunteers and other period garb.

Blue skies added to the festive mood on the streets, but even had the expected downpour happened, there was a sense that nothing would have kept the people away from this celebration. Like no other parade, it stirred a reawakening in our history felt by people of all walks of life from both home and abroad.

"It's great to be in Ireland during such an important event capturing the pride of a nation," said Emanuel Trindade from Portugal, who works in Dublin and attended the parade with his parents. I couldn't put it better myself.

We haven't had an Easter parade since the ending of *An Tóstal* (The Pageant), which ran for five years in the 1950s and came to an abrupt end when it failed to attract tourists during the Easter off-season. But yesterday's rousing parade wasn't put on for tourists, even though those who attended were treated to the warm Irish welcome for which we're renowned. This was for us and about us, the people of Ireland, and we loved it.

When the media is full of reports that half a million people are flooding into the city, you don't expect to run into an old friend at the bottom of Grafton Street, but I did.

"Where would you get an atmosphere like this?" he said. "To hear the Proclamation being read out brought tears to my eyes."

This from a hardheaded businessman not normally given to shows of emotion... but it was that kind of day, filled with emotion and cheer and a real connection with 1916.

It was a day when you were proud to be Irish, and we did ourselves proud too. Extra gardaí were drafted in, but things went more smoothly than anyone could have hoped for. We honoured the men and women of 1916, whose actions shaped the nation we live in today, and we did so with respect.

Even those who chose the occasion to protest did so with dignity. On Talbot Street, a group representing the homeless quietly handed out leaflets which read, "*One hundred years since the Easter Rising of 1916, we, the homeless families of Ireland ask that our children be cherished equally. There are over 1,800 children currently living in homeless accommodation today.*"

It was a poignant reminder that, in contrast to the jubilant sound of marching bands and cheering crowds, the reality of life for some of our citizens is a far cry from the ideals set out in the Proclamation of Independence. But the turnout at yesterday's parade may be the mark of a new engagement with those ideals.

171

Anne Kirwan came to me via Kerryman Micheál Ó Morain, an authority and biographer of Thomas Ashe, or Tomás Ághas, as he was born in Kinard in 1885. Having given me a one-on-one masterclass on the life and death of the patriot, Micheál put me in touch with the woman who now lives in the Dublin house where Ashe spent many years as a school principal. Micheál said she had a real connection with her predecessor and he was right: Anne told me she could sense Thomas Ashe in the walls. He was there from the very moment she set foot in the place, she said. I also spoke with his grand niece, Mairead Ashe Moriarty, who visited Anne on Easter Monday with other family members and said of her, "What a beautiful lady. We'll never forget the warmth of the welcome we received and how graciously she showed us Thomas Ashe's home."

'There's an Imprint of Thomas Ashe from the Energy in the Walls'

For most of the past century, Thomas Ashe remained a largely unsung hero of the Easter Rising, despite leading the most resounding rebel military success of 1916. But this week and in the coming months, the schoolteacher from Kinard, Co. Kerry, is being celebrated at a series of commemorations which began with a re-enactment of the Battle of Ashbourne, in which Ashe led the 5th (Fingal) Battalion of the Irish Volunteers to victory.

At a time when so many rebel garrisons were defeated attempting to hold static positions against overwhelming odds, Ashe and his men employed successful guerilla tactics in a fiercely fought action that in many ways foreshadowed the 'flying columns' of the subsequent War of Independence.

Although he was not among the leaders executed in the immediate aftermath of the Rising, Ashe died in equally controversial, if less well-remembered circumstances.

This story began two months after his release from Lewes Prison in June 1917, when Ashe was re-imprisoned having been arrested on the grounds of sedition, and held in Mountjoy. Denied prisoner-of-war status, he and other prisoners, including Austin Stack, refused to do any prison work. The authorities responded by stripping their cells and removing their footwear. Forced to lie on cold, damp floors, the prisoners went on hunger strike, in response to which they were force-fed.

At 11.00am on September 25th 1917, Thomas Ashe was strapped to a chair and an inexperienced medic, Dr Henry Lowe, pumped a mixture of milk mixed with raw eggs through a tube down his throat. Ashe collapsed shortly afterwards, and died that night in the Mater Hospital. A subsequent inquest reported he died of heart failure and congestion of the lungs and that the taking away of his bed, bedding and boots and allowing him to be on the cold floor for fifty hours, and then subjecting him to forcible feeding in his weak condition... was "an unfeeling and barbarous act."

Before the Rising, Ashe had been principal of Corduff National School in Lusk, Co. Dublin, and lived in the nearby schoolhouse. Today it's the home of Anne Kirwan, who says his energy lives on there to this day.

Ashe House is now known as a centre where Mindfulness and Self-compassion courses are run, and specialist training in the treatment of trauma is offered to psychotherapists, psychologists, psychiatrists, GPs and other healthcare professionals, as well as mindfulness and yoga courses for non-professional groups.

"Thomas Ashe is a powerful presence here," says Anne. "It's a place of True Refuge, and I hope that's what it was for him when he lived here too. At that time, Maud Gonne, Sean O'Casey, De Valera, Michael Collins and others were regular visitors. It's said that after a particularly lengthy meeting, one of them wrote 'Liberty Hall' on the glass panel of the front door.

"The moment we stepped through the gates, it was like stepping into another world. We immediately put in an offer and bought it. It's always been occupied by teachers.

"Today the house is still involved in education as a training venue, and my work is informed and influenced by Thomas Ashe's passion for growth and development. There's an imprint of the man in the energy from the walls. It's our family home, but it's also a space and place where people from all walks of life and traditions can open to their own growth and learning.

"I see myself as a custodian for those who have gone before. My vision has been to continue the sense of peace and calm that runs through the house and the gardens outside. We retained the original part of the house exactly as it was when Thomas lived here. It's a living history.

"As a man, teacher and revolutionary, Thomas Ashe had many gifts, including a love of people, Irish music, song, language, literature and culture. A great military tactician, he was against corporal punishment, an advocate for children with special needs, and set up the award-winning Black Raven Pipe Band in Lusk. I feel very protective of his memory and it saddens me to see him so overlooked in history to date."

But this year he was honoured with a series of events. On Saturday 30th April, the people of Kerry unveiled a plaque in his birthplace of Kinard, and another on a monument that stands to him in the centre of Lispole.

In Dublin, Aidan Arnold of the Lusk Heritage Centre wrote a play, *The Legacy of Ashbourne*, based on the transcript of the inquest into Ashe's death. With a special piece of music by the Black Raven Pipe Band, its performance by a local drama group was filmed in Swords Courthouse and screened in Corduff National School on Friday May 6th.

Members of the extended Ashe family were very pleased with the creative and dignified ways in which their relative was immortalised.

"The family couldn't be more proud of Thomas," says grand niece Mairead Ashe Moriarty. "He was an inspirational leader, a gifted educator and an extremely talented, kind and caring man. He was passionate about the Irish language, culture and traditions, and he had a vision for this country.

"We still have some of his memorabilia, like the seal skin on which his famous poem, '*Let Me Carry Your Cross for Ireland, Lord*' was inscribed in Lewes prison, and his bagpipes, both of which we donated to Dingle library for the centenary commemorations. He had a major influence on events that shaped our nation and it's wonderful that the country is honouring him and all the heroes of 1916."

In his poem, *Let Me Carry Your Cross for Ireland, Lord,* Thomas Ashe wrote one line which proved to be far from what transpired in reality: "*And few are the tears will for me fall, When I go on my way to you.*"

In fact, Thomas Ashe's death led to a marked rise in support for the Republican movement. His body lay in State at Dublin City Hall and his funeral attracted a turnout of 30,000 mourners from all over the country lining the streets as his cortege made its way to Glasnevin Cemetery on 30th September 1917.

Volunteers fired a volley in a graveside salute, after which Michael Collins delivered this short oration:

"Nothing additional remains to be said. That volley which we have just heard is the only speech which it is proper to make above the grave of a dead Fenian."

The public revulsion at the brutal manner of Thomas Ashe's death, and of the summary executions of the Easter Rising leaders, began to galvanise a nation.

For further information: www.ashehouse.ie

The business community in Dublin faced a double threat to their livelihood in 1916 - that of widespread looting, followed by fire and shelling from both artillery and the British gunboat the Helga steaming up the Liffey. Some businesses lost fortunes in looted stock, which subsequently took some time to reclaim in compensation from His Majesty's Government. Confectioners, jewellers, furriers, shoe shops, tobacco emporiums... all were considered fair game to the desperately poor people of Dublin. Many businesses never recovered from the devastation, but some rose from the ashes, even if it meant years of hardship before they received the money they needed to resume trading. And in the aftermath of the devastation, some savvy entrepreneurs saw the opportunity of a city in ruins to nab a bargain and became part of the rebuilding of Dublin.

Surviving 1916: Families Still in
Business a Century After the Rising

Easter Monday 1916 began as a peaceful, sunny day in Dublin, and for the shopkeepers, hoteliers and other city traders, it was very much business as usual.

Even when customers in the GPO were asked to leave the premises shortly after rebels seized the building at 12.20pm, their initial response was reported to have been more of bemusement than shock. Guests in nearby hotels sat enjoying their lunch, oblivious to what was about to unfold outside.

Few knew what lay ahead as the calm of the morning erupted into a violent frenzy, and the bustling city centre became a battle zone. The following report features five Dublin businesses caught up in the destruction of the city in 1916 who are still trading today.

McDowell's, the 'Happy Ring House'

Originally founded in Mary Street in 1870, McDowell's jewellers, more popularly known as the 'Happy Ring House,' moved to 3 Sackville Street in 1902, making it the longest standing business in one family ownership in O'Connell Street today.

"When the rebellion began, my late grandfather William tried to hold the shop as long as he could, for fear of looting," says manager Peter McDowell. "Eventually, though, it was too dangerous to stay, and he and the porter made a run for it from the premises to Cathedral Street, fifty yards away.

"In that short distance, the porter was shot dead and William received a leg wound and eventually made it home to Sutton by train from what was then Amiens Street station.

"After all that, the shop was looted and completely destroyed when the British gunboat, the Helga, sailed up the Liffey and bombarded the city. Eventually, William was reimbursed for looted stock by His Majesty's Government and the premises was rebuilt in 1917/18 using some original girders from the GPO.

"My uncle Jack McDowell succeeded William on his death in 1939, though he's perhaps best remembered for gaining notoriety in 1947 when his horse 'Caughoo' won the Aintree Grand National at odds of 200 to one.

"This was a highly controversial victory as it was reputed the horse completed only one circuit of the Aintree course instead of two, as it was a very foggy day and television coverage didn't exist.

"Now that my daughter Nicola has joined the family business to form the fifth generation, I'm confident the 'Happy Ring House' will continue to serve future generations of couples choosing their perfect ring before having a celebratory drink in the Gresham as has been a Dublin tradition for over a century."

Wynn's Hotel

Wynn's Hotel in Lower Abbey Street was the scene for some of the most important events in the nation's history. This is where Cumann na mBan was formed in April 1914, and where the first meeting of the Irish Volunteer Force was held. For decades Abbey actors, artists and literary giants hung out in its grand halls, and today's Relatives Association meet here to remember family members who fought in 1916.

On Thursday 27th April that year, under bombardment from British artillery, the hotel was destroyed by fire.

"A rebel Volunteer on the roof of the GPO later recalled how he saw '*men and women sitting in the windows of Wynn's Hotel watching the battle as from a theatre seat*,'" says sales and marketing manager Julie Loftus. "When the lives of guests and staff were threatened, they made their way under the protection of a makeshift white flag across Butt Bridge to the safety of its sister hotel, the Clarence.

"Wynn's was rebuilt in 1926, the first property in Dublin to use mass concrete for its construction. Plaques in the Saints and Scholars lounge mark the historic meetings that took place here."

Today Wynn's Hotel is popular with tourists and locals alike, many of whom say the ghosts of its past can still be felt today.

"Comedian Brendan O'Carroll filmed here recently and said it still has a haunted feeling," says Julie. "That's what makes it special – the place is full of character."

Barnardo Furriers

John Michael Barnardo opened his fur business in 1812, beside Dublin Castle, and later moved to Grafton Street where in 1916, it branded the royal crest as furriers to the British court. Today, Barnardo holds the proud boast of being the oldest furriers in the world.

John had nineteen children, thirteen with his first wife Eilis O'Brien, and five with his second, Eilis's sister Abigail. His most famous son, Thomas Barnardo founded the children's charity Barnardos 150 years ago. Having been refused a place at Dublin's College of Surgeons on the grounds that he was the son of a tradesman, Thomas studied medicine in London, where he was so moved by the plight of orphans after an outbreak of cholera in 1866, he set up his first children's home.

His brother Henry took over the furrier business, which today sees the fifth generation, Elizabeth and her mother Caroline manage the Grafton Street store. Caroline was married to Harry Barnardo for only seven years when he died from bone cancer, leaving her and their only child with nothing but loving memories and a thriving business to run.

"A family business like this is a bit like farming; you pass it on to the next generation," says Caroline. "Elizabeth was only six when Harry died and I tell her she was lucky to have had a father who loved her dearly and was really present in her life, if for only a short time. Wherever we went, Elizabeth came too. He used to call her his angel. He died thirty-eight years ago, and I'm blessed to have Elizabeth and her two beautiful children, Harry Junior and Elizabeth."

Mullen Sports

Joseph Mullen ran a successful business making bespoke leather shoes when the Easter Rising raged. Soon after the rebellion had ended, he bought a large site at the corner of Capel Street and Mary Street for the knockdown price of £3,000, and started trading in leather goods. Even in 1916, it was a bargain for a site of its size and location.

Born the same year, his eldest son, Joseph Jr grew up to become a keen footballer. When he was invited to play for

Huddersfield in the early 1930s, his father gave him the choice to follow his sporting dream – 'but know that we might never see you again,' he added – or take over the shop. Joseph Jr saw his mother crying, and said later, 'I couldn't do it.'

Instead, he combined both interests by turning Mullens into a sports shop. However, when his father died in 1947, the family was hit with a bill of £30,000 in death duties. Joseph Jr had to take out a mortgage and spent most of his working life paying it off. When he finally handed over the business to his son Alan, the current proprietor of Mullen Sports, he did so with the caveat, 'Never take a mortgage on this place, son.'

Alan heeded his father's sage advice, even during the boom years when credit was easy and it seemed everywhere he looked, people were investing in bank shares and building property portfolios. Such caution served him well when the Celtic Tiger gravy train screeched to a halt.

"Not taking a mortgage meant we were able to survive the crash," says Alan. "Dublin rents are tough for retailers, so to own the building is a great advantage. Mind you, we've had to change with the times. At one time Elverys and ourselves were the only sports shops in town, but in the early '90s, the big chains arrived and I needed to find a niche. I decided to specialise in martial arts and now I like to think Mullen Sports is the go-to place for boxing, judo and the other fighting arts, although we sell general sports equipment too.

"I may not be a millionaire, but thanks to my father and grandfather, I have a business, a career and a livelihood that's passed down through the generations for the last century, and hopefully it will still be here if my son Serge, now seven, chooses to join the family firm when he grows up."

John Brereton Jewellers

John Brereton is the third generation of his family to run the eponymous jewellery shop in Capel Street.

"My grandfather John Brereton bought the shop in Easter Week 1916. It was closed almost immediately as a result of the Rising, but opened again the following week. It was a pawnbroker's business then. There was a lot of poverty in Dublin and no government lending facilities, so people regularly pawned their personal belongings in return for cash to pay for living expenses. It was the social security of the generation, so to speak.

"In the 1930s my father Jack brought the jewellery business to the fore and now it's a real family enterprise. Specialising in both new and antique jewellery, the business has grown with the city. My brother Liam manages the shop in O'Connell Street, his son Derek and my son Paul run the Grafton Street store, and I'm here in the original building in Capel Street.

"Unlike other buildings in the city, this one escaped damage during the rebellion and the shop front looks pretty much as it did a hundred years ago. There's a preservation order on it now, because it's such an important part of the history of Dublin."

185

The Remembrance Wall (officially called the 'Necrology Wall') at Glasnevin Cemetery got off to a controversial start when it was unveiled on April 3rd. One camp objected to the inclusion of names of British military and police, while others argued that to ignore them would be to ignore fellow countrymen. Horns were still locked on the issue when a second rumpus erupted over a misplaced fada in the word 'Éiri.' No sooner had wreaths been laid than the stone mason was back at work quickly moving the fada from its incorrect position over the first 'i' to where it should have been over the 'E.' And then it was back to the names - or one in particular. While the wall was designed to remember all who had died as a result of the Easter Rising, including civilians killed in the conflict, one name appeared to be steeped more in mystery than history...

Mystery Surrounds Woman who Died on the Same Day as Pearse, Clarke and MacDonagh

A question mark has emerged over the true cause of death of a Kildare-born woman whose name appears alongside three of the Rising's best-known leaders on the newly unveiled 1916 Remembrance Wall.

Margaret McGuinness is among the hundreds of names - rebels, British military personnel and civilians alike - engraved on the wall to commemorate their fate as casualties of the fighting during Easter Week.

Her name stands out because she is one of only four people to be listed under 3 May 1916 - the same day that Proclamation signatories Thomas Clarke, Thomas MacDonagh and Pádraig Pearse were executed by firing squad after being sentenced to death by a British court martial.

Coming hard on the heels of protests against the inclusion of British soldiers on the wall, and embarrassment over a misplaced fada, however, research by the Irish Independent into Margaret's fate casts some doubt on whether she was in fact a casualty of the Rising.

Joe Duffy's online list of children killed in the Rising brings up a single-line entry beneath Bridget Stewart (11) of 3 Pembroke Cottages: "*Another casualty, Margaret McGuinness (54), who was killed in the Rising also had her address as 3 Pembroke Cottages, though there may have been more than one Pembroke Cottages.*"

And indeed there were, but Margaret didn't live in Number 3. According to the 1911 Census, Margaret's age was recorded as 54 and her husband Joseph, 51. Originally from Co. Kildare, they lived in 27 Pembroke Cottages, Pembroke West, a district that today takes in such areas as Ballsbridge, Donnybrook and Harold's Cross. Margaret's occupation was given as 'wife' and his as a 'general labourer'. They had no children, but they did have two young relatives living with them. Jennie, a niece, was 19 and working as a 'clerkess' in a commission agent's office, and Jack, a nephew, was an 11-year-old schoolboy.

Joseph died in 1914 and – well, we know when Margaret died. A death notice in the *Irish Independent* recorded: '*McGuinness Margaret, widow of the late Joseph, late of 27 Pembroke Cottages, Donnybrook, to Deansgrange Cemetery.*'

In the *Sinn Fein Rebellion Handbook*, which was printed in the wake of the Rising and documents events of the time, she is listed as being 50 years of age (considerably younger than her recorded age in the 1911 census) and having died as a result of "bullet or gunshot wounds."

However, according to her death certificate, issued on May 4th 1916, Margaret died from cerebral haemorrhage. The certificate doesn't elaborate or provide any further detail such as '*cerebral haemorrhage caused by gunshot wounds*,' it reads simply, '*Cerebral haemorrhage certified*.'

"Usually, when haemorrhage was caused by gunshot wounds or injury, the certificate would state, 'as a result of...' so it is a bit strange that it simply records 'cerebral haemorrhage,'" says Ray Bateson, author of books including *Deansgrange Cemetery and the Easter Rising* and *The Rising Dead* among others.

"I haven't come across any report of her death other than that reported in the newspaper. That's not to say that there isn't one; however, I would raise the query about the absence of gunshot wounds on the certificate. The location of death is not easy to make out, but the informant of the death is the occupier and the initials after appear to be SDU. This probably stands for South Dublin Union (now St James's Hospital), which raises more questions.

"A number of civilians were killed in the Union, which was occupied by the Volunteers during the Rising, and fierce gun battles took place there. But did Margaret McGuinness die locally, or at the SDU? And if the latter, did she die of natural causes or was she killed by gunfire?"

189

Handwriting expert David Madden of Document Examination Ireland says the location of death is unclear on the certificate.

"Under the date is something which could be a signature, or a place. It looks like the word ends in 'house' and it's followed by the letters SDU, as is repeated in the signature of the informant."

In 1916 the South Dublin Union was a sprawling complex of workhouses, hospitals and churches spread over fifty acres of land. Was Margaret injured in crossfire elsewhere in Dublin during Easter week and taken there where she died days later? Was she taken ill at home in Pembroke Cottages and rushed to hospital? Or had she been left destitute after Joseph died and ended up living in South Dublin Union, along with more than 3,000 others?

Was she wounded during the siege that followed the occupation of the SDU by the Volunteers, or was her cerebral haemorrhage an unfortunate but unrelated result of disease rather than injury?

Glasnevin Trust historian Conor Dodd says there's enough evidence to point to Margaret's death being, as recorded in the *Sinn Fein Handbook*, due to bullet or gunshot wounds.

"Civilians were caught in the middle of the fighting and many of those wounded died later of haemorrhage, which wasn't always recorded on their death certs," he says. "The balance of information is there to show she was a civilian casualty. Her death certificate is not a reason to discount her as a casualty of the Rising. There's nothing that says her death was conclusively not related to the Rising."

This is true. But neither is there conclusive evidence to show her death was related to the Rising. In the absence of any other records, it seems that the search for conclusive evidence about the cause of death of Margaret McGuinness has for now run into a brick wall, if not a marble one.

One of my first 'celeb' interviews as a young journalist was with the late singer Jim McCann, after his 1986 hit with the song 'Grace.' The romantic ballad is charged with emotion about the doomed marriage of Grace Gifford with Joseph Mary Plunkett hours before his execution; who couldn't be moved by the heartbreaking lyrics describing one of the saddest love stories of all time? Whatever Jim revealed during that interview, however, I couldn't tell you. We got so drunk, I had to call him the next day to help decipher my illegible notes. I do remember his dog was called Whiskey, after his favourite tipple, and the dog before that had answered to Brandy... Fast forward thirty years and now I'm chatting with the lovely Honor O'Brolchain, grand niece of Joseph Plunkett, who's setting the record straight about the cold reality of her grand uncle's wedding, and that famous song...

'Joseph Plunkett's Wedding Wasn't Romantic - It Was Sordid'

It's a love story that's been romanticised out of history and into legend and song. Following a whirlwind courtship, Grace Gifford and Joseph Plunkett married in his prison cell just hours before he was taken out to the Stonebreaker's Yard in Kilmainham Jail and shot for his part in the Easter Rising. When the late Jim McCann immortalised the star-crossed lovers in his famous ballad, '*Oh Grace, just hold me in your arms and let this moment linger...*' it brought a tear to the collective eye.

The song stirred emotions again when a live performance by family trio Danny O'Reilly, Róisín O and Aoife Scott in Kilmainham Gaol was a highlight of this year's acclaimed RTE *Centenary* concert. Yet in spite of its almost mythic status, there were no lingering embraces or touching of any kind during the actual wedding ceremony. Joseph and Grace were accompanied by an armed prison guard for the whole ten minutes they had to marry and say their final goodbyes. Consequently, the executed leader's family has mixed feelings about the song.

"I was embarrassed by it when it first came out," says Honor O'Brolchain, author, musician and grand niece of Joseph Plunkett. "However, everything it says is true and you grow fond of it after a while, and the *Centenary* performance was very beautiful."

In her book, *All in the Blood*, Honor reaches into the journals of her grandmother, Geraldine Plunkett Dillon, to bring to life a full-blooded, warts-and-all account of the relationship between Joseph and Grace.

Grace was one of six girls and six boys born to a wealthy Unionist family, with a Catholic father and Protestant mother. All the children were brought up as Protestants, although the boys were baptised as Catholics. However, Grace became a Catholic with all the devotion of a convert.

"Joe was on the rebound when they met," says Honor. "He'd spent five years completely infatuated with Columba O'Carroll, the subject of much of his poetry, but eventually she told him no more, and put and end to it.

"He then started working on a military plan for the Rising. His expertise in this area was respected by the older leaders, and it was he who devised the strategy for the successful Battle of Mount Street. During this time, September 1915, he met Grace and fell in love with her. They became engaged on

December 2nd and announced it in February. She was baptised a Catholic on April 7th.

"Joe asked her to marry him in Lent, but she said it didn't suit, as she'd be doing a Lenten ritual known as the 'Seven Churches.' She suggested Easter. He replied, 'I think we'll be running a revolution then.'"

There was another reason for Joseph's rush to the altar – he knew he was on borrowed time.

"Joe had glandular tuberculosis since the age of two or three," says Honor. "Shortly before the Rising, he had an operation and doctors gave him only a few weeks to live. For him, going out to be shot for Ireland was a far better end than dying of illness a few weeks later."

But there may have been a further compelling explanation why they ended up marrying hours before his execution.

"Fr Eugene McCarthy, the chaplain of Kilmainham, was said to have asked Grace: 'Do you have to get married?' She's supposed to have said yes.

"There was only one reason a couple had to get married in those days, and my grandmother's papers indicate that Grace was pregnant. It also explains why the jail governor granted permission for the wedding ceremony to take place."

Joseph may have hinted at their union in his poem, *New Love*, which begins:

'*The day I knew you loved me we had lain*
Deep in Coill Doraca down by Gleann na Scath.'

But it was his sister Geraldine who left the most telling clue to Grace's condition; she believed that her widowed sister-in-law was pregnant when she married Joseph, and had a miscarriage shortly afterwards. After the wedding, Grace was disowned by her mother, and Geraldine gave her a place to live in Larkfield, an estate in Kimmage owned by the Plunkett family.

"My grandmother wrote how she visited Grace in her bedroom one morning and found a large chamberpot full of blood and foetus. Neither woman said a word to each other about the matter."

Whether the miscarriage was induced, as some have speculated, we will never know. Shortly afterwards Grace went to America. In her book *Easter Widows*, historian Sinead McCoole notes that "six weeks after the wedding, Grace posed for a photograph in Chicago's *New World* newspaper wearing a white dress and fancy wristwatch, and holding a kitten. It was not the mournful air of the other Easter widows in their black weeds… but she goes down in the pantheon of Irish heroines as the great love of his life."

Their relationship aside, Joseph was an astute military strategist, and profoundly aware of the power of propaganda. It was at his behest that his father, Count George Noble Plunkett went to Rome to visit the Pope before the Rising.

"Rome had bestowed the papal title on George when he donated a house to an order of nuns. This gave him the right to an audience with the Pope, which he did not to seek the Pope's blessing for the Rising, but to ask him not to condemn it.

"George's wife, the Countess, handled domestic matters. She was known to be a strong, formidable woman, and she denied Grace the inheritance she felt she was due as Joe's widow. In 1935, Grace took a case against the Plunketts, which they settled out of court for £700."

Grace Gifford, a talented artist and cartoonist, never remarried. She died suddenly, and alone, in Dublin on 13th December 1955, and was given a military funeral attended by President Sean T. O'Kelly.

On May 4th this year, the Plunkett family unveiled a plaque to Joseph Mary Plunkett at 26 Upper Fitzwilliam Street, where he grew up.

All in the Blood, from the memoirs of Geraldine Plunkett Dillon, edited by Honor O'Brolchain, first published by A&A Farmer, is soon to be reissued by the O'Brien Press, who also published *16 LIVES: Joseph Plunkett* by Honor O'Brolchain.

Sometimes you set out to cover one story and wind your way round to another... Stephen National Treasure Dunford had intrigued me about a play called 'The Spancel of Death' that had been scheduled to open in the Abbey Theatre on Easter Tuesday 1916. However, due to the small matter of an armed rebellion raging outside, the show was cancelled. The play, by T.H. Nally, was a tale of witchcraft in which a strip of skin from a human corpse was used to create a love charm that no man could resist. But not only did the show not go on, The Spancel went on to become known as 'the play that never played.' Why? I spoke with the Abbey archivist Mairéad Delaney, who recounted stories about the theatre before, during and after the Rising with such enthusiasm that I was soon intrigued as much by the players as the play, and in particular, the somewhat strident theatre manager.

A Front Row Seat
at the Theatre of War

On Easter Monday 1916, Abbey Theatre manager St John Greer Ervine had a front row seat for the real-life drama unfolding on the street outside, as rebels marched the short distance from Liberty Hall to the GPO.

Ervine was preparing for the matinee of *Kathleen Ni Houlihan*, the play by WB Yeats and Lady Gregory depicting Ireland as an old crone transformed into a beautiful young queen when men die for her.

As the first shots rang out from the GPO at about 1.15pm, Ervine realised the show would go on – but not in the confines of his beloved theatre. In the ultimate case of life imitating art, this production was happening for real, and the martyrdom of its leading men would soon garner a global audience for a tiny nation taking on the might of the British empire. As Kathleen proclaims in the play, "*The people shall hear them forever.*"

"Ervine, a staunch Ulster Unionist, shared none of the nationalist sympathies of many of his players," says Abbey archivist Mairead Delaney. "Fearing '*Kathleen*' would play into the hands of the rebels and further incite the people, he cancelled all performances that week."

First on the cast list of *Kathleen Ni Houlihan* was Sean Connolly, who would go on to mark other 'firsts' as he led his troop of ten men and ten women to Dublin Castle, the headquarters of British administration in Ireland. He was the first rebel to kill a fellow Irishman, Constable James O'Brien, at the castle gates, and the first of the rebel fatalities when he in turn was shot dead on the roof of City Hall.

Connolly died in the arms of fellow Abbey actor Helena Molony, a prominent republican, feminist and labour activist who'd spent the previous night in Liberty Hall with a parcel of printed copies of the Proclamation under her pillow.

The company's original leading actress, Maire Nic Shiubhlaigh was a key member of Cumann na mBan, and took charge of the women in Jacob's biscuit factory, while actor Arthur Shields fought in the GPO. Arthur's brother William was better known by his stage name, Barry Fitzgerald, who went on to win an Oscar for his role in *Going My Way* (1944).

"On Easter Sunday Arthur returned from the Abbey's English tour," says Mairead. "On the Monday, he got permission to drop off a script at the Abbey before reporting to

James Connolly at the GPO. It's believed to have been the script for *The Spancel of Death*, a story of witchcraft by Mayo playwright T. H. Nally, which was to premiere on Easter Tuesday. Actors were never given an entire script in those days, as it was too expensive to print. Instead they were given only their part.

"After the Rising, Arthur served time in Frongoch prison in Wales, but he was back treading the boards that September, and went on to become a Hollywood star in the 1930s. To this day, *The Spancel of Death* has never performed by the Abbey and is now known as 'the play that never played.'"

Arthur Shields starred with his brother Barry in such movies as *How Green Was My Valley* (1941) and *The Quiet Man* (1952), and he featured in a number of 1960s TV series such as *Wagon Train, Rawhide* and *Bonanza*.

But it wasn't just the Abbey actors who were active in the Rising; many behind the scenes were also involved. Prompter Barney Murphy fought in the Four Courts, and usherette Ellen (Nellie) Bushell, was stationed at Jacob's factory, as was stage hand Peadar Kearney, who wrote the national anthem.

Between the nightly curfew imposed immediately after the Rising, and the fact that many of its key players were in prison, the Abbey Theatre didn't reopen for some weeks and when it did, relations between the manager and his players were strained, to say the least.

It wasn't helped by Ervine announcing his biggest regret of the Rising was that the British naval ship the Helga didn't train her guns on the Abbey and blow the theatre sky high.

"That was partly because the British Government would issue compensation for buildings damaged during the insurrection and owners could use the money to expand their premises," says Mairéad. "Apart from a couple of smashed windows, the Abbey remained intact, perhaps infuriatingly for Ervine."

When he put actors on notice for not turning up for rehearsals, they went on strike and the company temporarily disbanded. Ervine enlisted with the Dublin Fusiliers and fought in Flanders, where he lost one of his legs in the conflict. In later years his disdain for southern Irish became more pronounced; in a letter to George Bernard Shaw, he described Ireland as brimming with "bleating Celtic Twilighters, sex-starved daughters of the Gael, gangsters and gombeen men."

But the vast majority of Abbey staff supported nationalism, republicanism and women's suffrage at the time of the Rising. In her research into the history of the theatre, Mairéad noted a preponderence of poets, playwrights, actors and behind-the-scenes staff who were revolutionaries. There was no mistaking the political message in many of the plays and literature of the time, and the entire Abbey team, from actors to usherettes, playwrights to prompters, were certainly exposed to radical ideas in the course of their day-to-day work.

"I wonder how much of what they saw here might have helped to radicalise them," says Mairéad. "Part of the mission of the Abbey Theatre since it opened in 1904 was to put the deeper thoughts and emotions of Ireland on the stage, and I wonder if that influenced the people who worked there. Did art inform their political beliefs?"

Undoubtedly, tales of heroic nationalism were part of the cultural revival that went hand in hand with the political revolution of the time, but nobody could have foreseen the accuracy of some productions that had been put on years before the Rising took place.

"For instance, rebel leader Thomas MacDonagh's play, *When the Dawn is Come*, which premiered in 1908, was set in the future, at a time of insurrection, and featured seven captains of the Irish Insurgent Army," says Mairéad. "And in 1913, a play ironically called *The Post Office* translated by Yeats from Indian poet Rabindranath Tagore's work, dealt with themes of liberation from captivity.

"Conscious though I am of looking back now with twenty-twenty vision, I often wonder if it was with some kind of prescience that these plays predicted such detail of what was to happen years later."

"Who told you about the ghosts?" Artist Liam O'Neill's response to my question about whether he ever got a sense of the ghosts of 1916 making their presence felt took me by surprise. We were talking about his 'Visionaries of Ireland' exhibition, which included portraits of the Rising leaders alongside those of Irish literary greats, all painted in the artist's uniquely bold and breathtaking style. "I didn't mean literally," I said, "just, you know, a feeling..." "But it's not just a feeling," he went on, "I see them every day, as real as any living person. They don't leave me alone. They're with me during the day, they follow me upstairs at night, and when I sleep they haunt my dreams. How did you know about the ghosts?" Well, I didn't. But even if Liam's pals in the pub in Corca Dhuibhne told him to go away outta that with his ghost stories, I was all ears.

How the Ghosts of 1916 Haunted
Kerry Artist Liam O'Neill

He's painted the Boss twice, both Springsteen and Haughey, as well as farmers, fishermen, horse fairs and the lush landscapes of his native Kerry, but it wasn't until his house became haunted last year that renowned artist Liam O'Neill turned his easel towards 1916.

He had no choice, he says. Having completed a series of paintings of great Irish writers, from Beckett, Shaw, Yeats and Joyce right up to Francis Stuart and Seamus Heaney, he was ready to take a break from portraits for a while. He fully intended going back to capturing the wild, rugged fields and mountains, harbours and seas of his birthplace Corca Dhuibhne, in the riot of colour and bold palette-knife strokes that he's made his own.

But for a man not normally given to flights of fancy, he was surprised by a persistent and other-worldly insistence that he wasn't yet finished with the dead poets' society. Other late luminaries wanted face time with the artist, and if he wasn't going to listen to his heart, they'd have to make him sit up and take notice. They still do.

"The ghosts of the Easter Rising patriots are all around me," he says. "They're everywhere, hanging around the walls of every room, and if I try and get away from them in the evening, they follow me upstairs.

"They stand around my bed at night and when I sleep they haunt my dreams. They've taken over my life completely in the last year."

The haunting began about a year ago, at first emerging as stray thoughts which crystallised and gathered momentum as time went on.

"It started as I was coming to the end of the writers project, the centenary was approaching and I couldn't stop thinking that the 1916 patriots were poets, playwrights and writers too, visionaries all. I have no doubt that if Sean MacDiarmada, Thomas MacDonagh and Thomas Ashe had lived, they'd have taken their place among the literary giants of this country."

"The more I thought about it, the more it made sense to me to combine their portraits with those of the writers, and so I started to paint.

"Straight away, I could see them clearly before me; I still do. I study their faces, their eyes, their hair . . . Tom Clarke is the only one with a receding hairline, and I'm the only one in the room with grey hair. They're full of colour."

His pals down at the local pub in Corca Dhuibhne are having none of it. When he starts on the subject, he says they'd rather leave their pint on the counter and call it a night than listen to more of his 'ghost stories.' But Liam knows how to deal with his ethereal friends.

"I know that if I ever hear them talking to me, I'm in trouble," he says. "I talk to them all the time, and so far they haven't answered me back. I left the hardest two till last. Dev and Collins are the most recognisable characters, but in the end, they flowed more easily than the others."

They also took shape a lot faster than his famous last portrait of Charlie Haughey, completed shortly before his death in June 2006. When a mutual friend suggested to the former Fianna Fáil leader that Liam should paint his portrait, Haughey said: "Send him over."

Liam likes to get to know his subjects before putting paint to canvas, but even he didn't anticipate how long this picture would take to begin, never mind end.

"Every Thursday for two-and-a-half years, I called over to Kinsealy at 11am and walked around talking to Charlie, and it took me two years to even start the portrait," he says. "We were like two neighbours from West Kerry. He'd ask, 'How's my friend Paidí Ó Sé?' And we'd be off again, chatting about people and places we knew.

"We never discussed politics. I'm not political and these

were just friendly, private meetings. He was a changed man.

"Eventually, I realised I had to concentrate on the portrait. I painted him in a casual, open-necked shirt, a marine jacket, his hands are visible, and his eyes are looking downward, perhaps reflecting. His widow Maureen has the painting in her home."

Largely self-taught, Liam now ranks among Ireland's most talented contemporary artists, and his work is collected nationally and internationally. Before he became a full-time artist, Liam was a special needs teacher at a school in Dublin and painted in his spare time. He says he's cautious by nature and was in no hurry to give up the day job. It wasn't until he had twenty exhibitions under his belt that he did so.

"Let's just say, I was reared safe," he says. "As the thirteenth out of fourteen children, you wouldn't be quick to relinquish a secure living. The truth is, though, I loved teaching kids with special needs. I still do."

It's this passion which brought him, in a roundabout way, to his exhibition being shown this year at the Irish Consulate in New York, an experience he says was the result of "a fantastic coincidence."

When Jean Kennedy Smith, sister of the late Robert, Ted and John F Kennedy, was US Ambassador to Ireland from 1993 to 1998, she attended an art class given by Liam to his students with special needs. This was something close to the then Ambassador's heart and she was so impressed, she invited the students to exhibit at the US Embassy, and so began a long friendship between the artist and the diplomat.

Smith is the founder of Very Special Arts, an international non-profit organisation that encourages people with disabilities to engage with the arts.

"This year, she invited me to do some workshops in New York in May, and that led to my 'Visionaries of Ireland' exhibition tying in with that," says Liam.

According to the Government centenary programme, "In this exhibition, Liam O'Neill is saluting all those writers, dramatists, poets and revolutionaries who played their part in turning life's waters into wine during the late years of the nineteenth and the early years of the twentieth century. The visionaries who, for one reason or another, weighed so lightly what they gave, as Yeats put it."

The show, which opened at the Oriel Gallery in Dublin before heading Stateside, contains twenty-five portraits and one stunning landscape depicting the West Kerry Volunteers crossing the Conor Pass on Easter Saturday 1916.

"They marched from Ballyferriter towards Tralee, joined by other Volunteers on the way, only to be told when they got there that the Rising wasn't going ahead, and they dispersed. I wanted to capture their passion as they made that arduous journey with the very best of intentions to fight for their country."

If he saw their ghosts too, he didn't flinch from the suffering of ordinary men and women enduring rain and biting winds to reach their goal, and then to be told to go home.

Learning about such stories has been a voyage of discovery for Liam, who says he came to the project with little knowledge about the Rising and, especially, what followed.

"Personally, the Easter Rising means more to me today than it did a year ago. I've got to know the personalities involved. They were young and idealistic, they had a vision for Ireland, and they loved the Irish language, a passion I share with them today.

"When I was at school, history stopped at 1916. What happened afterwards was too painful and even after decades, too raw to face, for fear that bringing it out into the open might risk rubbing further salt into the wound.

"The brutalities that happened in Kerry and elsewhere during the Civil War were so traumatic, schoolteachers in my time simply avoided modern Irish history. As children, we knew more about Joan of Arc than Countess Markievicz. Now, one hundred years after the Rising, I'm blown away by the nature and breadth of the commemorations.

"I've admired President Michael D. Higgins all my life, but this year of all years, he's the right person in the right place."

Having moved from Dublin back to Kerry in 2002, Liam is in no doubt that he too is in the right place. Now settled in an idyllic part of the Kingdom where he can enjoy the unspoilt landscape that inspires so much of his work, indulge his love of Irish language and culture, and all with the added benefits of success and international acclaim, he may well be living the dream of the very ghosts he's brought to life on canvas.

"Being here is like living in paradise," he says. "As for the acclaim, sure – after thirty-two years, I'm an overnight success."

Hanging out in cemeteries may not seem like everybody's idea of fun, but author Ray Bateson feels right at home walking among the dead. Ray is no tombstone tourist, however; he has documented so much history from consecrated grounds that he's a foremost authority on the cemeteries of Ireland and their occupants. Having first spoken to him about the mysterious Margaret McGuinness whose name appeared on the 1916 Remembrance Wall, I was keen to talk to him about his fascination with the Rising Dead (also the title of one of his books). His vast knowledge has come from years of sustained, methodical, passionate and relentless mining of information from Irish burial grounds. And the man is well named, because he's shed a Ray of light on a great number of hitherto forgotten casualties of the Easter Rising, who can now take their proper place in the annals of history.

Celebrating Unsung Heroes
on the Graveyard Shift

The unveiling of the Remembrance Wall in Glasnevin Cemetery was one of the most solemn events of this year's centenary commemorations, an occasion for sober reflection as a group of children drew back the curtains to reveal the names of 485 people who died in the Easter Rising.

Yet according to a leading authority on the subject, the Remembrance Wall is controversial not only because it includes the names of British military personnel; he claims it excludes many of those entitled to have their names engraved for posterity.

Author Ray Bateson says his biggest concern is for the forgotten heroes of the Rising – those whose names don't appear on any memorial plaque or monument, despite evidence

213

to show they were active in the rebellion. He also wants to correct those listed as civilian casualties, who actually died fighting for their country.

"The official list we have today was drawn up fifty years ago, but we've got more information since then, and new ways of looking at things," he says. "The military pensions scheme distorted the original list. Take Patrick Lynch, for instance, whose sister was denied a pension, even though two eyewitnesses reported seeing him killed in Moore Lane after the evacuation of the GPO.

"Ernest Cavanagh, a cartoonist, was killed by a sniper's bullet as he stood unarmed on the steps of Liberty Hall on Easter Tuesday. He's mentioned in *The Last Post*, published by the National Graves Association, but not in any other list."

Ray's interest in the subject goes back over a decade, when his work gave new meaning to the term 'graveyard shift.' In the early days of his research, he'd pack a picnic lunch and spend all day in a cemetery, poring over graves of Volunteers, civilians, policemen, doctors, nurses, children… anyone and everyone whose life ended as a result of the rebellion of 1916. He took notes, compared what he found with what was already documented, and slowly, painstakingly began building a clearer picture of the Rising dead.

To explore their lives, he found no better place to start than with their final resting place.

"Much of our knowledge of the ancient world comes from burial sites," he says. "How, when and where people were buried is a very important part of our understanding of civilisation, and it's long been an interest of mine. So ten years ago, I thought I'd do a little booklet looking at where 1916 Volunteers were buried."

That turned into a book, *They Died by Pearse's Side*, the first in a series by Ray whose other publications include *Memorials to the Rising*, and *The Rising Dead: DMP and RIC*.

"The plaque at Arbour Hill lists sixty-two Volunteers in addition to Roger Casement and Thomas Kent, but there's sufficient evidence to show that over seventy Volunteers were killed. In the past, the timescale for establishing the cause of deaths from such an event used to be a year and a day, but that's no longer relevant.

"Volunteer Joe Brabazon died in 1929, but the cause of death was lead poisoning due to gunshot wounds sustained during Easter 1916. Surely he deserves to be categorised as a casualty of the Rising?

"We need a proper investigation by a panel of experts who will apply modern criteria to devise a definitive list. It should include a special mention of those who lost their lives and remain unknown, like the Unknown Soldier.

"I also believe that medical personnel deserve a special category. They were more than civilians, given that they went out to save all those injured in the fighting – civilians, volunteers and policemen alike.

"Nurse Margaret Kehoe, based at the South Dublin Union, was shot dead when she rushed outside to administer first aid to a wounded rebel. At an unveiling of a plaque to her at St Kevin's Hospital in 1965, Joseph Doolan, who had fought at the SDU recalled Éamonn Ceannt saying after her death in 1916, 'She died for Ireland just as surely as if she had worn the Volunteer uniform.'"

One of the most remarkable stories uncovered by Ray is that of John Neale, a London-born socialist who joined the Irish rebels in the Rising and was wounded while serving as a lookout in the Metropole Hotel. Stationed with him was Volunteer Charles Saurin, who described Neale as "one of the calmest and bravest individuals I have ever encountered."

In an article published in 1926, Saurin wrote: "*During the heavy firing he used to sit right out on the parapet which ran past the window of the top floor and scan the whole street with a pair of field glasses, apparently quite oblivious of the fact that any moment might be his last.*"

On the Friday, Neale, known to his fellow insurgents as 'Comrade,' was badly wounded and carried to Moore Street.

"*All the lower part of his body was riddled and though his wounds were attended to at once it was obvious that it was only a matter of time till his end,*" wrote Saurin.

"*He lasted till the next day and I learnt afterwards that he died as he was being carried into the Castle Hospital. This London Cockney, as I believe him to have been, was one of the bravest and coolest of men and deserved a better fate. I do not think he ever got recognition in the casualties lists which were published later.*"

Such recognition for Neale and others is long overdue, according to Ray Bateson.

"The Easter Rising was the catalyst that won us our freedom. We need to acknowledge the valiant efforts of all those who fought without a care for themselves so that future generations would be free, and equally, those medics who lost their lives in the crossfire."

Three books by Ray Bateson - *They Died by Pearse's Side*, *Memorials of the Easter Rising*, and *The Rising Dead: RIC & DMP* - are all available from www.therisingdead.com

At Liam O'Neill's exhibition in Dublin's Oriel Gallery, singer and storyteller Noel O'Grady delivered a hauntingly beautiful performance. His voice, whether speaking in his irresistibly soft Kerry accent, or singing a capella in honeyed tones, had guests mesmerised. When he explained how the lyrics of certain songs would have resonated in the context of 1916, and then sang them for us, there was much dabbing of eyes among the spellbound gathering. Such sweet music delivered a powerful emotional response and there was nothing for it, I had to collar this man and ask him to talk to me about how and why he connected with the Easter Rising. Just as I did, a reporter from TG4 simultaneously scrambled for his attention. Noel switched effortlessly from English to do the TV interview 'as Gaeilge' and back to English again for me. I was won over by this talented entertainer.

'The Easter Rising?
I'll Sing to That'

You don't have to be descended from someone who fought in the Easter Rising to feel a connection with this key event in history. Singer, raconteur and retired Irish Army Commandant, Noel O' Grady stakes his claim to 1916 as enthusiastically as anyone with a direct bloodline to the rebels.

"I don't have a relative, but I have a passion," says the man who's spent much of this year commemorating the event at venues big and small, from a cosy pub outside Trim, to Listowel in his native Kerry, Áras an Uachtaráin at President Higgins's invitation, and the centre stage of the rebellion itself, the GPO on Easter Monday.

He's also been invited to perform in Kolkata (formerly Calcutta) in 1919 in celebration of Easter 1916's influence on

India's insurrections and eventual independence.

"I hadn't planned on being involved with the commemoration activities," he says. "If anything, as a former weapons instructor, I had an underlying sense that if I ever saw a gun, or even an image of a gun again, it would be too soon.

"Then the 1916 Relatives Association asked me to perform in the GPO. I finished with *The Soldier's Song*, which most of the GPO rebels sang on Friday evening in the burning building whose roof was about to cave in."

It's not just the lyrical quality of his tenor voice that has audiences captivated. Whether he's singing *as Gaeilge*, or breathing new life into old standards, it's as much his stories between songs that bring the music, poetry, art and culture of a hundred years ago to life. An award-winning singer, he's won many fans by bringing a lump to the throat of a new generation with his heartfelt rendition of old classics.

"As I sing *There's No Place Like Home*, I think of the executed leaders of the Rising and their bereft loved ones," he says. "Home resonates with people facing death.

"When a gun was put to my head during a UN tour in El Salvador in 1993, my only thought was of home, and that knock on the door...

"James Connolly's last thoughts were also of home. During his wife Lillie's final visit, he urged her to entrust his poems, plays, songs, and other works to Francis Sheehy Skeffington to sell, in the hope it would keep the wolf from the family door. She had to break the news to him that Skeffington had been executed during Easter Week."

Noel also relates to Roger Casement, who spent years in the Congo and Peru exposing the human rights violations of slaves in the rubber plantations. During his army career, Noel's final overseas posting was to the Congo, where he contracted malaria.

"I recovered quickly thanks to modern medicine. Casement and the slaves he championed endured far worse, yet he later managed to negotiate a shipment of armaments from Germany for Easter 1916. He was physically exhausted as he struggled onto Banna Strand, his dreams sunk with the arms, yet he subsequently was said to have walked like a prince to the gallows."

The Volunteer scheduled to pilot the Aud into Fenit Harbour, Murt O' Leary from the Maharees in west Kerry, was a neighbour and friend of Noel's mother, 91-year-old Eileen O' Grady. Noel's father Harry, a member of An Gárda Siochána, was stationed in several Kerry towns with links to the Rising. Noel himself was commissioned into Cathal Brugha Barracks where Skeffington was executed and where Michael Collins lived until ambushed at Béal na Bláth.

James Joyce's *Portrait of the Artist as a Young Man* whose centenary is this year, also resonates with Noel whose one-man show: *Ode to James Joyce: Portrait of a Tenor* tours worldwide. Joyce attended Irish language classes given by Padraig Pearse.

"Art for me, in all its forms, is about connection," says

221

Noel. "The same is true of leadership. And though as a military man I'd question some of the strategies of the Rising leaders – locking themselves into buildings and not expecting to be artillery-shelled, for instance, and digging in Stephen's Green without first controlling any of the surrounding buildings – I'm in awe of their valour and vision.

"For them, the Rising was a sea change in a gradual path for freedom. James Connolly exemplified this in his 1903 composition, *A Rebel Song*, which features the stirring and prophetic line, '*Our march is nearer done, with each setting of the sun.*'

"What his and his comrades' heartfelt plea was: this isn't simple, it will take time, there will be twists, but our blood sacrifice will further the cause for future generations.

"One of the central figures of the Fenian Rising of 1867 was Westmeath-born John Keegan Casey, whose pen was mightier than his pike. Just a teenager when he wrote *The Rising of the Moon*, he died on St Patrick's Day 1870, mainly from punishments sustained in Mountjoy Prison. In his short twenty-three years, he helped prepare the fuse that ignited in Easter 1916."

Noel remembers these heroes in the haunting lament, *Táimse Im' Chodhladh*, an 'aisling' or dream poem.

"Momentous events don't just happen, they're caused – by artists, dreamers and visionaries," says Noel. "The dreams and defiance of these visionaries paved the way. As Yeats said, 'It was the dream itself enchanted me.'

"For centuries, we couldn't express our mother tongue, our religion… we could only dream.

"As an artist and military man with over thirty years' service, I'm fascinated with 1916. And when I watched with pride our still fledging sovereign country's Easter commemoration parade through the streets of Dublin this year, I saw democracy on the march. On seeing troops currently serving overseas, I remembered the likes of Tom Kettle and Francis Ledwidge and all others who died, and those who returned home. As a young independent nation, we've come a long way."

Noel O'Grady's album *The Enchanted Way* is available from www.noelogrady.com

Having been granted an interview with Dr Diarmuid Martin, I arrived at the Archbishop's House, a large, red-bricked Victorian building in Drumcondra on Dublin's Northside. While waiting in a high-ceilinged room traditionally furnished with a desk, bookcases, armchairs and coffee tables, I mused whether, as an atheist, I should address him as 'Your Grace,' or would 'Doctor' suffice. Moments later, he swept into the room with a cheery smile and I knew it wouldn't matter. The diocesan communications director sat to the side, politely informing me of another appointment the Archbishop had in thirty minutes. No problem, I said. I'll be out of here, promise. An hour later I left, mulling over on the way out how down-to-earth, warm, intelligent and great fun the Archbishop had been, and I was in no doubt that 'Your Grace' was indeed the appropriate term to address such a lovely, gracious man.

Archbishop Diarmuid Martin: 'Why is the Catholic System Not Delivering What it Should?'

From the time he was a boy, Archbishop Diarmuid Martin was enthralled by his mother's early recollections of 1916. Eileen Mullen was only a little girl at the time, living in the Coombe in the heart of Dublin, yet the gathering clouds in the city were so heavy with foreboding, even children could sense that something momentous was about to unfold.

"My mother's first memory was watching her mother putting bullets into a bandolier for my uncle Martin, who was part of the Jacob's factory garrison," he says. "I often wondered how she could do that, watch her son go out to kill, or be killed."

Martin survived and was quickly dispatched with his fellow rebels to Frongoch prison in Wales. But while one brother had gone out to strike a blow for Irish freedom, another had already left to serve his king and country in the First World War.

"The second oldest, James, had run away and joined the British Army," says Dr Martin. "His father wanted his sons to move into his building firm as bricklayers, but James didn't want that, so he fled. He was wounded in Gallipoli and lost the sight in one eye, and only returned to Ireland in 1938, a few days before his mother died. He worked in the British Civil Service until he retired, while Martin ended up as the Chief Inspector of dangerous buildings in Dublin."

The women in the family were also active in the cause. One sister joined the Irish Citizen Army, and another Cumann na mBan, and their mother was not afraid to speak her mind.

"Once, when two British soldiers and two RIC people came to raid the house, my grandmother let the British soldiers in, because they were working for their country, but not the RIC people, as she felt they were doing jobs which were not suitable for fellow Irish men and Irish women," says Dr Martin.

"I was brought up to be proud of my relatives who played their part in the Rising. I can't separate myself from my family participation in it and inevitably the commitment of one generation is passed on to another.

"It's always a difficult task to see how you justify violence. Most of us are pacifists in our hearts, but you have to understand the frustration there was in Ireland at that time. Whether they really expected a prolonged military combat, I just don't know, so it's very hard to judge."

If the Catholic hierarchy at the time didn't outwardly support the planned violent rebellion, only a small minority of bishops actually condemned it. Bishop Patrick Foley of Kildare instructed his priests not to give absolution to the rebels in confession if they were willing to kill for their cause.

Not all bishops of the era were so censorious, however. Edward Byrne, who became Archbishop of Dublin in 1921, allowed priests to absolve people who died in the city's brothels.

"Mind you, it was on condition the bodies were brought to the front door, so the priests wouldn't witness the inner workings of these houses of ill repute!" says Dr Martin.

The majority of bishops in 1916 were not in favour of the Rising, but was there a difference in attitude between the priests of the diocese and those of the religious orders?

"The clergy on all sides were divided," he says. "The Capuchins were nationalistic, but then there were the anti-Rising priests known as 'Castle Catholics' – that is, Catholics who frequented Dublin Castle. The priests in the Pro Cathedral ministered on both sides of O'Connell Street. On one side was the GPO; on the other, one of the worst slums in Europe, and not just in the human condition, but in the moral condition."

If the clergy was divided, so too was the vast majority of civilians at the time.

"The people living in the slums weren't out on the streets cheering on the rebels," he says. "At the very most they were interested in survival. And the people at the races were not particularly interested either. But within months of the shooting of the leaders, public opinion had changed dramatically."

Not only did the executions galvanize support worldwide for the Irish cause, they left an indelible mark on both the priests who witnessed them, and the soldiers who carried them out.

"There was almost a tenderness in the way the young soldiers had to blindfold the men before they were shot," says Dr Martin.

"The priest who witnessed the shooting of James Connolly described Connolly slumping so badly in a chair, he was instead put on a stretcher and propped up against a wall, and the way he was shot, the blood came out everywhere, so you could imagine how traumatic that was. The chaplain at Arbour Hill said the bodies arrived still warm, their mouths open, blood dripping from them, and they were thrown into a mass grave.

"The brutality of the immediate reprisals – and it wasn't just General Maxwell acting as an individual; he obviously had clear instructions that there were to be no negotiations whatsoever about this process – rebounded to a great extent on future history."

While Archbishop Martin reflects on the past, he's also asking hard questions about the future. After decades of sexual scandal and cover-ups, vocations to the priesthood in freefall and a generation of young people rejecting the faith of their fathers, this is a pivotal time in the history of the Catholic Church.

"If we accept the Proclamation as a document of ideals, we have to ask where are those ideals today, and where have we failed?" he says. "I think, one hundred years later, it means asking ourselves where we're going – not looking back, but asking the Catholic church in particular to take stock of that idealism. Does idealism still exist, or has it been neutralised by the cynicism of what we've seen happen in Ireland?

"Most of our young people who have gone through up to twelve years of Catholic education don't end up practising Catholics. You have to ask why the system is not delivering what it should.

"It's a logical question to ask, yet some people see any criticism of the Church as anti-Catholic. It's not. The Catholic Church in Ireland needs to carry out an honest appraisal of its place in Irish society in the future, otherwise it risks being trapped in its own history.

"We've achieved great things, but there's a fragmentation in Irish society now and you have to ask, where do we look for leadership, especially for young people?"

He's just turned seventy-one, older than any of his aunts and uncles ever lived, but he's in rude good health. While he says, "Yes, we're living longer, but you don't want a country run by octogenarians," you're left in no doubt that, as long as Dr Diarmuid Martin is in the driving seat, he'll face the challenges of his Church with one eye on the rear view mirror, but his gaze is fixed firmly on the road ahead.

Mary MacBride Walsh has every reason to be proud of her family's close connections with 1916. The grand niece of Major John MacBride and cousin of international humanitarian Seán MacBride, she spoke about them so eloquently and with such love and passion and humour, I adored her from the start. My original plan was to feature both Mary and a fellow Westport-onian Seamus Gavin together about an upcoming commemoration event in their town, but the two stories screamed to be written separately. So that's the way this cookie crumbled. While trying to be demographically inclusive, sometimes you get two great standalone stories from the same town and I wasn't about to sacrifice either one for the sake of geographical correctness. I do wonder though if there's something in the Mayo air that imbues its people with storytelling magic.

A Nation Once Again

In 1916, Irish people had come to dread the knock on the door. So often it heralded unwelcome news – a loved one killed either here or on the battlefields of Europe, or shipped off to prison somewhere far from home.

For Honoria Gill MacBride, the knock on the door at her home in Westport came not from an officer or a gentleman, but an eleven-year-old boy.

Having seen the morning headlines, a local newsagent had dispatched young Tommy Hevey to break the devastating news that Honoria's youngest son, Major John MacBride, had been executed by firing squad.

John, the estranged husband of Maud Gonne, had been second in command to Thomas MacDonagh in Jacob's biscuit

231

factory during the Easter Rising. As he was led out to the Stonebreaker's yard in Kilmainham Jail on May 5th 1916, he refused to wear the blindfold offered him. Having fought the British in the Boer War years earlier, he said, "I've looked down the muzzles of their guns before."

But Honoria's troubles weren't over yet. Days later, another son, Joseph MacBride, and his first cousin Joseph Gill were among a group of Mayo men arrested and interned in England and Wales. One of the last prisoners to be released, Joseph didn't arrive home until Christmas Day that year.

He went on to become the first elected Sinn Féin MP for Mayo West two years later, while his nephew, Seán Mac Bride, only son of John and Maud Gonne, would go on to become a distinguished statesman, Assistant Secretary General of the United Nations, founder of Amnesty International and winner of the Nobel and Lenin Peace Prizes for his human rights achievements.

"Seán received ten honorary doctorates throughout the world, but none from Ireland," says Mary MacBride Walsh, granddaughter of Joseph.

She and Seán were closely related, because not only were his father and her grandfather brothers, his mother and her grandmother were also half-sisters.

"When Colonel Thomas Gonne's wife Edith died at the age of twenty-eight, Thomas had an affair with the governess Margaret Wilson, which resulted in the birth of Maud's half-sister, Eileen," she explains. "Joseph MacBride married Eileen, and his brother John married Maud, so two brothers married two half-sisters."

John and Maud split acrimoniously a year after their son was born. In a separation agreement, Maud won custody of the baby until the age of twelve, and she raised him for those years in Paris. John was granted visiting rights and one month each summer.

"My grandparents spoke fondly of John's visits home, when he'd bring sweets and regale them with stories of the Boer War," says Mary. "He was godfather to his niece Sheila Durcan, mother of the poet Paul Durcan."

Seán never took sides in his parents' separation and, to the delight of the MacBride family, once he was of age, he sought them out and visited often. For years, he and Mary made an annual pilgrimage to Arbour Hill Prison to pay their respects to his father and the other executed Rising leaders in their final resting place. She also spent time in Seán's Dublin home, entertaining a global A-list of his close friends.

"You never knew who'd be sitting next to you at his dinner table – Bishop Desmond Tutu, Kader Asmal, Anthony Cronin, Bono, Mary Robinson, Mary McAleese... Seán was an extraordinary man, highly intelligent, a dedicated human rights activist, and a very caring man with a great sense of humour."

With her experience of entertaining world dignitaries, Mary was the perfect choice to host President Michael D. Higgins and his wife Sabina at a 1916 commemoration day in Westport. Over 1,500 people gathered in the town on May 8th 2016 to remember their local heroes. The sun shone right on cue as the ceremonies began with the unveiling of a plaque at the John MacBride monument to thirty-one Westport men interned in 1916.

The monument bears an inscription of Major MacBride's own words, from his address on the Manchester Martyrs in 1914: *"No man can claim authority to barter away the immutable rights of Nationhood; for Irishmen have fought, suffered and died in defence of those rights. And, thank God, Irishmen will always be found to snatch up the torch from the slumbering fire, to hold it aloft as a guiding light, and hand it on, blazing afresh, to the succeeding generation."*

In his commemoration speech, President Higgins noted, "The people of Mayo were never slow to stir and we're here today to celebrate that sense of coming together in public to defend what is principled."

Stirred herself by the emotion of the day, Mary read the Proclamation in a moving tribute that brought the words of Padraig Pearse to life for a new generation.

"It was a joy and a privilege to read the Proclamation on such a special day," she says. "It was one of those moments that makes you stop and think about those noble and courageous heroes who gave their lives for Ireland. I could almost hear their voices as I began to read, '*Irish men and Irish women: In the name of God and the dead generations…*' It's a tremendous document. I love every line of it."

The event in Westport was more intimate but no less

234

rousing than the national commemoration in Dublin on Easter Sunday this year, which Mary attended with her husband, five children and extended family.

"Relatives who'd come from Chicago and Nebraska were blown away by the ceremonies," she says.

"To be in Dublin on Easter Sunday, witnessing the dignity and discipline of the defence forces, listening to *The Parting Glass* as the tricolour flew in the wind, to hear the Proclamation being read out from the GPO and see the flyover from the air corps... It was a spine-tingling, unforgettable, once-in-a-lifetime experience.

"For me, there's no doubt that without the Easter Rising, Ireland would still be occupied. I'm proud to be related to Major John MacBride, who gave his life to break the stranglehold Britain had on the country for the previous seven hundred years, and I think everyone should be equally proud of him and all his comrades."

Seamus Gavin's story about his relatives highlighted for me not only how political passions a century ago tore families apart, but how communities too were blighted in the aftermath of the Rising. Today we take the premise of 'innocent until proved guilty' for granted. Back then one brother could have another jailed on hearsay only. Imagine the atmosphere of fear, mistrust, suspicion, anger and bitterness that must have descended on every town and village across the land. Then add to that an influx of prisoners released from the 'University of Revolution' that was Frongoch, newly graduated in areas of military strategy, weaponry skills, cultural identity and a determination to break free from the oppressor. Think about that and you can see the toxic mixture coming to boil, ready to erupt into an almighty explosion that would reverberate through generations to follow.

'Civil War Began in Our Family
Long Before 1916'

If Dublin was the epicentre of the seismic activities of the Easter Rising in 1916, its immediate aftermath sent shock waves that spread to every corner of the land. Under the orders of General Sir John Maxwell, reprisals came thick and fast.

The executions of the leaders were followed by a nationwide hunt to purge the country of subversive elements. Within weeks, more than 3,000 people were arrested and over 1,800 interned without trial.

This was payback time and the authorities were determined to quash any further attempt at rebellion. Suspicions of seditious activity against Britain provided sufficient grounds for arrest and internment. Blatant unruliness incurred harsher penalties, as 21-year-old Luke Sheridan from Castlebar discovered when he was heard to shout on a sunny July day, 'Up the rebels!' That infringement earned the young man eighty-four days imprisonment with hard labour. The sentence was later reduced to twenty-eight days when local MP William Doris issued an appeal on his behalf.

However, Doris made no such intervention for his own brother Patrick Joseph, who was rounded up with thirty other locals and packed off to the remote camp of Frongoch in Wales, a training ground for freedom fighters that became known to its inmates as 'Ollscoil na Réabhlóide,' or 'University of Revolution.'

But why journalist PJ Doris was arrested was baffling: not only had he not supported the uprising, he'd written strongly-worded editorials condemning it. And why did his brother not plead his innocence?

Seamus Gavin, first cousin twice removed, sheds light on the estranged Doris brothers, who this year had a bridge named after them in their home town of Westport, Co. Mayo.

"William and PJ were devout nationalists who founded the *Mayo News* together in 1892," he says. "They set up the newspaper to give a voice to the Irish cause and published countless articles attacking British government policies, particularly those that kept Irish people locked in landlordism.

"The eldest and more experienced of the two, William became the first editor, having already written for a number of national newspapers. However, he and PJ disagreed strongly over their differing views on nationalism.

"William was a stringent Home Rule man, a close friend of Michael Davitt and John Redmond. Having helped draft the 'No Rent Manifesto' for the Land League in 1881, he was charged with 'compelling persons to abstain from rents lawfully,' and sentenced to six months in prison.

"PJ was also immersed in the Land League movement, but didn't support Home Rule. For him, nothing short of a completely independent country with its own parliament would suffice. When William was elected to parliament in Westminster as Nationalist MP for Mayo West, PJ took over as editor and used the paper to support the increasingly popular Sinn Féin party.

"However, despite PJ's political stance, he didn't believe an armed rebellion had any chance of succeeding. The local Volunteers willing to fight in 1916 were so desperately short of arms, all they could actually do during Easter Week was march around the town."

That show of defiance had the police follow them and take their names. On their subsequent arrest in May, most didn't know what offence they were being charged with, only that they were detained under the spurious 'Defence of the Realm Act,' and held in Castlebar before being sent to Dublin and from there, put on board the cattle boats to Britain.

But if PJ had never supported an armed uprising, why was he punished for it?

"It's possible that William orchestrated his arrest," reveals Seamus. "There was no reason for PJ to have been interned,

239

but PJ vehemently maintained that William tipped off the authorities, accusing his brother of being a subversive."

In a letter to Dublin headquarters on May 14th 1916, Colonel BP Portal of Castlebar described PJ Doris and five others as "*the most dangerous Sinn Feiners in Westport district.*"

The pair who had started out as partners in print were now deadly enemies. PJ was brought to Richmond Barracks in Dublin, before being shipped to Stafford prison and then on to Frongoch. Finally transferred to Reading prison, he wrote daily letters to the prison governor, protesting his innocence and accusing William of having had him interned. He was finally released on Christmas Day, 1916.

He and William never spoke to each other again.

"The Civil War began in our family long before it broke out in the country, although both brothers strongly opposed partition," says Seamus. "The first serious rift arose when William supported Irish men volunteering for the British Army in WW1, but PJ's arrest and internment caused a schism.

"Then in 1918, William lost his seat to the Sinn Féin candidate who was supported by PJ through the *Mayo News*. It was the final nail in the coffin. They never reconciled.

"William moved to Dublin and died in 1926. His body is buried in an unmarked grave in Glasnevin. PJ died in 1937 and is buried locally. Thankfully, the conflict between the two brothers did not pass down through generations. It was a pleasure to meet nieces, nephews, cousins and other relatives, including William's granddaughter Mary, who came together for the recent naming of the Doris Brothers' Bridge in Westport.

"William and PJ clearly had their differences, but they both made a great contribution to the cause of Irish freedom, and I'm proud that neither shot anyone as a result of their beliefs. To have a bridge named after them as a public memorial in this centenary year is really fitting, because a bridge symbolises hope and unity, connecting two sides that would otherwise remain divided.

"The brothers may not have sorted out their personal differences while they were alive, but I'm very happy that they've left a great legacy behind."

A relative of Ned Daly, Kathleen Clarke and other activists of the era, biographer Helen Litton comes from a family steeped in the history of 1916, but you won't find her wallowing in any kind of reflected glory from that. Raised by a pacifist mother to oppose violence as a means of resolving disputes, she grew up with conflicting views about the Easter Rising. This ambivalence has given Helen a calm, measured and considered insight that enriches her discussion about the events, characters and repercussions of 1916. When we spoke, she reflected on the kind of Ireland the rebels of that time had hoped to create, and how different it is from the one in which we now live; how democratic the centenary celebrations have been; and how enthusiastically people across the country have connected with the Easter Rising in this centenary year.

'The 1916 Celebrations Have Helped
People Connect on a Personal Level'

The spectacular parade through the streets of Dublin on Easter Sunday last was not, after all, the culmination of the 1916 commemorations; it was just the beginning. As centenaries go, this one appears to have captured the imagination of Irish people like no other, and we're in no hurry to let it go.

With festivals, concerts, dedication ceremonies and countless other events planned in towns and villages nationwide over the coming months, Easter Rising fever shows no signs of abating.

Nobody is more surprised by this turn of events than Helen Litton, grand niece of Edward 'Ned' Daly and Kathleen Clarke, and author of two books about 1916.

"The level of interest people have shown has been

astonishing," she says. "It strikes me as a new generation reclaiming this important part of history. Almost every school in the country now has a 1916 corner with pictures and poems and stories written by the children. It's like a series of miniature museums.

"This has been an incredible year – and it's not over yet. Communities continue to put on their own local events, and mark the centenary in their own way, thanks to small grants that have made the commemorations very democratic."

The 1916 Relatives Association, of which Helen is a member, are happy that their ancestors are being remembered in this way.

"The association was set up to honour all who had fought in the rank and file in 1916 to be honoured, not only the leaders. I've spoken at numerous events, and met families inspired to research their own links who discovered things like Granny's old Cumann na mBan uniform in the attic. People have really connected on a personal level, and engaged with this part of our history with surprising enthusiasm."

Her own family connection has been well documented. At twenty-five, Ned Daly was the youngest leader to be executed, having commanded the 1st Battalion in the Four Courts. His sister Kathleen, a founding member of Cumann na mBan, married Tom Clarke, a man twice her age who had served fifteen years in jail for his part in a campaign to bomb London.

"Tom Clarke is one of the forgotten leaders," says Helen. "If Pearse was the poster boy for the Rising – a clean-living,

Catholic schoolmaster – Clarke was seen as an insignificant shopkeeper with a murky past. He worked behind the scenes, so he got overlooked to a large extent in the official history."

He's been remembered this year, however, with Dublin's East Link Bridge having been renamed the Tom Clarke Bridge in his honour. However, Helen reveals her mother, 91, did not approve of Clarke or the Rising.

"My mother is a pacifist who sees armed rebellion as pointless violence and an utter waste of life. She used to say the leaders were misguided, and whatever about the younger men, she had even less time for Tom Clarke, an old Fenian who, in today's terms, might be considered a terrorist. She didn't encourage any discussion about the Easter Rising when we were growing up.

"I'm ambivalent about it. For me, it wasn't the Rising itself that changed the course of history, but the British reprisals that followed in its wake.

"Had the leaders been jailed for a few years and then released, perhaps no one would have remembered them as anything other than a pack of fools, but they were more than that. These were men of strong feelings, and I'm proud to be related to two of them.

"However, when I look at Ned Daly, only twenty-five years old when he was executed, I wonder would it not have been better to have lived, and helped to build a new Ireland?"

It's this kind of reflection that differentiates this centenary year from the fiftieth anniversary in 1966.

"The tone then was triumphalist and militaristic, and of course, the Troubles in the North a few years later put a stop to that. There's a different mood this time, one that's more mature and considered."

She remembers her grandfather making the trip from Limerick to be part of the fiftieth anniversary in Dublin, one of the few times when he reminisced with the family about 1916, "but it was the funny stories he shared, not the painful ones. His generation had too many sad memories.

"This year has been a catharsis, it's brought the events of 1916 back into focus, the good and the bad, but we have some very difficult years ahead. After the Civil War, silence descended on Irish families and I believe it still hasn't lifted. How we commemorate that, I just don't know. Painful memories will have to be discussed, and atrocities remembered. This was brother against brother, and those things carry on for generations.

"I prefer to focus on the stirring sentiments of the Proclamation, to look at the kind of Ireland that these people hoped to see, which is very different from the country we live in today."

Helen has also put a lot of energy into the Save Moore Street campaign, which got a boost in May this year when a High Court judge refused to allow any further work on the site, and declared it should be a national monument.

"We were over the moon to hear the judge declare Moore Street a battlefield site, but it will have been a pyrrhic victory

246

if nothing is done to save it. This needs to be made into a historic quarter, where people can walk along and see the bullet holes, see where the O'Rahilly died, and where the bodies of civilians lay on the street, provoking Patrick Pearse's surrender.

"Moore Street is where the surrender took place, not the GPO. We need to safeguard this site for future generations to treasure."

Helen Litton is author of *Edward Daly* and *Tom Clarke* in the series *16 Lives*, and editor of Kathleen Clarke's autobiography, *Revolutionary Woman*, all published by O'Brien Press.

As a boy, Fr Hugh MacMahon minded his manners when Aunt Sorcha came to visit. He remembers her as a formal figure, not very talkative, and certainly not given to sharing fond reminiscences about the old days. Imagine his surprise then when he started researching his family history - and discovered the tight-lipped aunt he knew had once been an intrepid Cumann na mBan activist who cycled round Dublin with guns in her basket and escaped almost certain capture only when marriage allowed her to change her name and go undercover. And there was more... his own father had drilled with Tom Clarke and Uncle Peadar fought in Stephen's Green and Jacob's biscuit factory. "I could hardly believe it!" says Hugh, whose story reflects so many of those who got more than they bargained for when they started digging into their own family links with 1916.

'The 1916 Secrets
My Father Kept Hidden'

Brian MacMahon was a young Volunteer eager for action in 1916, but a bout of scarlet fever crushed any dreams he had of fighting for his country. Instead he spent Easter Week in Hardwicke Street Hospital, where he listened to the battle rage right outside the window.

'*Bullets smashed the windows of the ward and once into the wall a foot from my head,*' he wrote in his journal. '*It was maddening to be there in bed listening to the firing.*'

His confinement was a blow for the boy who'd come from Coas, Co. Monaghan to Dublin to study law in UCD and worked for Tom Clarke, running errands and drilling with the Rising leader at every opportunity. Clarke was so impressed, he handed the boy a gun to carry in the St Patrick's Day parade that March. He would have been carrying another at Easter had illness not interrupted his dreams of glory.

As soon as he recovered, however, Brian threw himself into the cause and was active in the War of Independence, until a bomb attack in Dundalk left him severely injured.

"He was a semi-invalid for the rest of his life," says his son, Fr Hugh MacMahon, who only recently discovered the extent of his family's involvement in 1916 and the eventful years that followed. Brian's brother Peadar fought in Stephen's Green before rejoining his own battalion in Jacob's biscuit factory.

"Peadar was interned in Frongoch, and in 1920 he was arrested in an attempt to bring guns from Dublin to Cavan, and imprisoned in the Curragh, where he was elected Prisoner Commandant," says Hugh. "He later became Chief of Staff of the Defence Forces and served as Secretary at the Department of Defence from 1927 up to the Second World War."

And then there was Sorcha, the boys' sister, on the surface a genteel bookkeeper with a fiancé in tow, but behind the façade she was a committed activist who routinely carried guns hidden in her bicycle basket and delivered messages from the GPO, ignoring the many dangers she faced.

Records show that Sorcha left the GPO for various locations over fifty times during Easter Week, during which time she was a direct link between Proclamation signatory Tom Clarke and his wife Kathleen, Sorcha's best friend.

"Sorcha was a main mover in Cumann na mBan," says Hugh. "I discovered that late one night before Easter, she met

Tom Clarke and his friend Sean McGarry, to receive a pistol Sean had for her. While they chatted, Sean started fooling around and pointed the pistol at Clarke, who told him to stop messing with it. McGarry assured him it wasn't loaded and pulled the trigger. But the gun was loaded and just as it went off, Clarke stepped to the side and received a bullet wound to the right arm.

"Had he stood still, it would likely have pierced his heart. As it was, he had to practise shooting with his left hand in the days leading up to the Rising.

"Sorcha postponed her wedding to fiancé Tom Rogers because she knew the Rising was planned, and they waited till November that year to get married. Her new name enabled her to drop out of police files as she continued her undercover work delivering messages and guns."

It was a far cry from the elderly aunt who in later years would visit her brother Brian's family in Blackrock, Co. Dublin from her home on the other side of the city in Howth. Hugh remembers Aunt Sorcha as "a formal presence" and "not a loquacious woman." It was only in recent years that he discovered a very different side to the father, aunt and uncle he thought he knew.

"After fifty years in the Orient, I came home from China and Korea three years ago and began to research my family's involvement in the Easter Rising," he says.

"A cousin directed me to a journal my father had written, and as I read it I could hardly believe my eyes. There were thirty pages in all, stuff he'd never shared with his family.

"He first met Rose while he was on the run in the home of his fellow officer Patrick Finegan, but after the explosion, he'd given up on dreams of marriage; because of the injuries he sustained, he didn't think any woman would be interested.

"Years later, Rose's brothers gave her a little ribbing about whether she'd ever settle down and she said, 'The only man I'd marry is Brian MacMahon.' So they got them together again around 1930."

Brian and Rose went on to have five children, two of whom became nuns and Hugh a Columban missionary priest.

After the Rising, Sorcha worked with Kathleen Clarke who set up the Irish Republican Prisoners' Dependents' Fund. Kathleen appointed Michael Collins to administer the funds on his release from Frongoch.

"Sorcha worked closely with Collins through the War of Independence and stayed with him on the pro-Treaty side, while Kathleen was firmly anti-Treaty," says Hugh. "These were complex relationships, but even though they were on opposite sides, Sorcha and Kathleen never let the Civil War destroy their friendship."

Inspired by these stories, Hugh decided to put together a record for the family. The result is his book, *A Fist to the Black-Blooded*, a family motto that means 'Resistance to the Oppressor.'

"Who knows why the three siblings from Coas were prepared to risk their lives for the freedom of their country?"

he says. "Some people simply live out the spirit on a wider canvas, and from what I knew of them growing up, they were most humble about it."

A Fist to the Black-Blooded: The MacMahons of Coas by Hugh MacMahon is available from Easons of Monaghan Town.

Paul Callery is relentless in his pursuit of recognition for his grand uncle Willie Halpin. Through his research, Paul discovered Willie suffered from what we now understand as Post Traumatic Stress Disorder after his participation in the Rising and subsequent internment in Frongoch prison camp. Having tried to take his own life there, Willie was transferred to Denbigh Asylum, Wales and from there to what was then known (abhorrently in today's terms) as Grangegorman Lunatic Asylum. He died there in 1925 and it's unlikely we'd have heard of him again were it not for the tenacity of his grand nephew. I was moved by the poignancy of this story, not only because of the heartbreaking sadness of Willie's tragic end, but for the pride, compassion and love a relative shows for him a century later. For me, this is a tender familial love story that transcends time.

Fear and Foreboding in Frongoch,
the 'University of Revolution'

In June 1916, 1,800 Easter Rising rebels from various British prisons were marched under armed guard on to trains and transferred to Frongoch internment camp in North Wales.

Frongoch, until then used to detain German prisoners of war, would play a critical role in the ensuing War of Independence. It was here that influential figures like Michael Collins, Arthur Griffith, William Cosgrave and others planted the seeds of further rebellion in the minds of receptive young men for whom the camp became known as '*Ollscoil na Réabhlóide*,' or 'University of Revolution.'

But while the internees learned about strategy and guerrilla tactics, they did so in appalling conditions. Those in the North Camp were crammed in cold, damp wooden huts, while those across the road in the South Camp found themselves in rat-infested rooms with poor ventilation.

Freezing, hungry and not knowing what was to become of them, many prisoners struggled to cope with their internment. One who fared particularly badly was Willie Halpin, a 23-year-old pork butcher who'd fought in the City Hall garrison in Easter week.

"Willie suffered what we know today as Post Traumatic Stress Disorder," says his grand nephew Paul Callery, a former artillery soldier. "Rumour has it that he was standing next to Sean Connolly when Connolly was shot in the head. That in itself would have been a shocking thing to experience, but just a few hours later, he was asked to take over a building across the road.

"He and his fellow Volunteers were under intensive sniper fire from Dublin Castle and Dame Street, and at first they couldn't get into the building, but Willie broke his rifle bashing through the door and they gained entry and later reported back to City Hall. Three days later they surrendered."

Willie's cousin John Halpin took part in the occupation of the Four Courts and the GPO during the Rising and was also interned in Frongoch – he in the South Camp and Willie in the North. But while John managed to keep up his spirits as best he could, Willie was not so fortunate.

"Willie suffered terrible beatings from the prison guards," says Paul. "He was so troubled by the events of 1916 and conditions in Frongoch, he became suicidal. Soldiers are trained to take advantage of weakness and it's possible those in charge saw him as vulnerable and bullied him. And despite the beatings, Willie did not receive the medical help he needed.

"Doctors in the camp were under orders not to treat patients who refused to give their names, but one of them, Dr Peters – the same doctor who attended Willie and failed to treat him – broke under the strain and drowned himself in a nearby river."

He wasn't the only one who broke. On August 3rd, Willie tried to cut his own throat, and was transferred to North Wales County Lunacy Asylum in Denbigh. When he returned to Ireland in 1917, he was confined in the Richmond Lunatic Asylum in Grangegorman, where he died in 1925.

"The word 'lunatic' was used right up to the 1930s," says Paul. "There was no history of mental illness in the family, and it's heartbreaking to think this man who took up arms and clearly suffered PTSD as a result of what he witnessed both during the Rising and in his time in Frongoch, came to such a sad end. His mother Mary wasn't the same after it."

Willie's cousin John was released from Frongoch in December 1916. Four years later, he was involved in a riot in Dublin after a memorial mass for Eamonn Ceannt and suffered brain injuries when the RIC baton-charged the protestors. He was taken to hospital and a steel plate was inserted into his head.

"In 1934, he developed headaches and was taken to Grangegorman," says Paul. "The same year, he was awarded a medal and a military pension of £20 a year.

"However, on his death in Grangegorman in 1938, the family had a hard job to get his pension paid to them. At that time, pension payments depended on who was in power. Whether they were pro- or anti-Treaty, they tended to favour their own; others would have to wait.

"John's funeral cost £26, including the white robe he was buried in, the coffin and the grave in Glasnevin cemetery. But his father was worried they'd have to exhume the body and bury him in a pauper's grave, because they didn't have the money to pay for it. Eventually, John's pension came through and the family could stop worrying.

"Willie, on the other hand, never received a pension or, more importantly to my mind, a medal to recognise the role he played in the Rising, but I haven't given up trying. It may be one hundred years later, but I'm determined to get that medal to honour the sacrifice he made.

"The people who fought in 1916 took on one of the biggest empires in the world and they all deserve recognition for that."

As a member of the Dublin Brigade Irish Volunteers History Group, Paul has visited Frongoch a number of times and describes it as a 'spiritual place.'

"The atmosphere is really poignant," he says. "I walk around it with a sense of pride, knowing that this is where the War of Independence really began.

"We're going back at the end of 2016 to mark the centenary of the last prisoners to be released. It's a symbolic trip and, for us, an important one. We want to take them home."

For the record, there were two Willie Halpins who fought in City Hall in 1916. The website irishmedals.org lists one as *William Halpin, Irish Citizen Army, born 1890, died 16th February 1951, aged about 26 years old during the Rising; fought in City Hall. He was arrested by the British Military on Thursday and taken to Dublin Castle Hospital suffering from exhaustion; he had gone without water for several days. He was interned until December 1916. On release he re-joined the Citizen Army and took part in the War of Independence...*

It also lists another William Halpin (Paul's grand uncle) as *William Halpin, Irish Citizen Army; fought in City Hall and the GPO... was subsequently interned. Due to illness, William Halpin was transferred from Frongoch Internment Camp, Wales, to Denbigh Asylum, Denbighshire, Wales in 1916 and later to Richmond Asylum (Grangegorman Mental Hospital), Dublin in 1917. Mary Halpin, his mother, claimed for a pension but was unsuccessful as cases of mental disabilities did not come under the scope of the Military Service Pensions Act, 1923. William died before the legislation was changed and a new application could be made.*

Against all odds, Fergus O'Kelly managed to transmit the world's first radio news broadcast during the Easter Rising. What a feat that was, considering the obstacles that stood in his way. He had to mobilise a team to get through a sealed telegraphy school, reconstruct communications equipment that had lain dismantled for two years, dodge bullets while running between that building and the GPO across the road, and try to get a message to the world that Ireland had declared herself a republic. It was Joseph Mary Plunkett, a man who understood the importance of communications, who had given the twenty-year-old the order. Can you see anyone taking on such a mission today? It's insane! Yet Fergus accomplished his mission, the message was picked up and word got to America... No wonder his relatives are bursting with pride a hundred years later.

Ground Control
to Radio America

The chaos and carnage of central Dublin at the height of the 1916 Rising might seem like a world away from the 'Madmen' glamour of American advertising in the '60s, but no less an authority than media guru Marshall McLuhan provides an unlikely link between the two.

Often credited with predicting the worldwide web decades before it happened, McLuhan was famous for his industry defining expressions such as '*the medium is the message*' and '*the global village.*'

Less well known, however, is a passage in his 1964 book *Understanding Media*, in which he pinpointed the world's first radio news broadcast to Dublin during the Easter Rising.

McLuhan wrote: '*The Irish rebels used a ship's radio to*

make, not a point-to-point message, but a diffused broadcast in hope of getting word to any ship that would relay their story to the American press. This is widely accepted as the world's first radio broadcast.'

It was a feat of monumental proportions. Less than fifteen years after Marconi sent the first radio signal across the Atlantic via link stations in Wexford and Galway, wireless communication was in its infancy. The telegraphy school in Reis's Chambers at the corner of Abbey Street and O'Connell Street had been shut down and sealed by British authorities at the outbreak of World War One in 1914, and the equipment dismantled.

Yet under orders from Joseph Mary Plunkett, 20-year-old engineering student Fergus O'Kelly overcame these hurdles to let the world know that Ireland had declared herself a republic. Having set up an aerial on the roof, with gunfire raging all around, he and his team began to relay the message in Morse code on Tuesday morning, as instructed by James Connolly:

"Irish Republic declared in Dublin today. Irish troops have captured city and are in full possession. Enemy cannot move in city. The whole country rising."

"It was not possible to get in direct touch with any station or ship, but the message was sent out on the normal commercial wavelength in the hope some ship would receive it and relay it as interesting news," Fergus recalled in his military witness statement in 1950.

They continued to send this and other messages at regular

intervals until the following day, when the building came under such heavy sniper and machine-gun fire that they had to abandon the transmission and make their way to the GPO.

While the rebels had no way of knowing if their message had been received, it was in fact picked up by a transatlantic ship, which is said to have relayed it to America, where newspapers reported details of the revolt before the official British version of events got out.

Paula O'Kelly is enormously proud of her late father-in-law's achievements.

"I was surprised he survived the Rising, because he had to make so many trips over and back between Abbey Street and the GPO," she says. "He and the six men on his team, including Abbey actor Arthur Shields who went on to become a Hollywood star, had to run zig-zag across O'Connell Street to escape the firing, which came at them from all directions."

Paula, who sadly lost her husband Michael, Fergus's only son, twenty-five years ago, has been researching the family history for over twenty years. After the Rising, Fergus was sent to Stafford Jail, where he celebrated his twenty-first birthday on June 1st.

"His mother sent him a white shirt for the occasion, and most likely enclosed some food as well," says Paula. "It wasn't the most auspicious way to mark a special birthday, but no doubt was very well received."

Days later he was brought to Frongoch camp in Wales and at the end of July was transferred to Wormwood Scrubs and released. He walked from the boat in Dun Laoghaire to the family home in Stillorgan, a changed man.

"At first the family barely recognised this emaciated, bearded figure looking in the window but they were overjoyed to have him home," says Paula.

But Fergus didn't stay in Stillorgan for long. Due to his internment, he had missed his final college exams and was determined to succeed at the repeats. A busy suburban house packed with thirteen children (he was the second eldest) and two parents was not exactly an atmosphere conducive to study, so he took off to the Dublin mountains and camped in the wilderness, with only his books for company.

Graduating later that year with a Bachelor of Science, he subsequently completed a degree in electrical and mechanical engineering and then went on to work in the Shannon electrification scheme.

This year Paula and her family were invited to the official commemoration ceremony in O'Connell Street on Easter Sunday.

"I'll never forget it," she says. "Though it wasn't planned, we ended up sitting right outside the GPO, facing what is now the Central Bar – the very building where Fergus had set up the radio transmission. This made the event particularly moving for us."

While Paula's father-in-law earned a place in the history books for his role in the Easter Rising, her own grandfather, John Middleton, was a constable in the Royal Irish

Constabulary. He was based in Tipperary and retired in 1903 after thirty years' service.

"Technically, that meant he would have been on the other side of the fence, so it would have been fascinating to hear his own views on the rebellion," she says. "Unfortunately, it was not to be as my grandfather died in 1922, so we can only speculate."

I'd expected 'My 1916' to end at Easter, but due to popular demand of all things related to the centenary (no, not only my series, thank you all the same), it continued till the end of June. I asked the features editor if I could sign off with my own take on what the Easter Rising meant to me. Thank you Liz for saying yes, because before embarking on this project, 1916 was just another so-what date to me, and now it means so much. I finally have an appreciation of how one event, led by so few, changed the lives of so many, and its repercussions have reverberated right up to this day. Thank you to all who shared your stories and helped me to see 1916 through your eyes. I could see the people you told me about, hear their voices, imagine myself in their shoes... For me they're neither heroes nor villains, but real, ordinary people who did extraordinary things. Here's to the ghosts of 1916.

My 1916:
An Education

Like many Irish people of a certain age, I did not grow up with a love of history. Penal laws, the Reform Act… So many dates, so little to capture a young girl's interest.

Whoever drew up the curriculum in the 1960s and '70s may have had the best intentions when he – for you can be sure it was a he – decided that no school leaver could be expected to function in the modern world without a good working knowledge of the Land League of the 1880s.

But where were the women *fadó, fadó*? Judging by the textbooks, there weren't any. The clue was in the name – his story.

"How did you find the history paper?" asked my subject teacher Mr Carty at the Leaving Cert school graduation dance in St Laurence College Loughlinstown in 1977.

"I didn't bother sitting it, Sir," I announced proudly.

"Oh, Miss Naughton!" he sighed.

So when the *Irish Independent* asked last year if I'd be interested in writing a series called '*My 1916*' in the lead up to the centenary commemorations, I had to 'fess up. All I knew of Padraig Pearse was seeing his face on a postage stamp, on the back of which I could have written everything I'd ever learned about the Easter Rising. However, I know a good story when I meet one, and as the subtext to the series was 'W*hat the Easter Rising means to me*,' I was hooked. If I could find out how people connected with 1916 on a really personal level, that's when the story would tell itself. And it did, in ways I never imagined.

"Tell me everything you know about the Easter Rising; I've got a series to write," I said to my husband Jan, who happens to have a passion for history.

When I'd peeled him off the floor and he'd given me a masterclass in *Stair na hÉireann* for dummies, answering my inane questions with minimal rolling of the eyes (e.g. "*The RIC - they were British, right?*"), I set about finding people with interesting stories to tell.

It wasn't hard. Artists, writers, business people, homemakers, singers, teachers, actors, priests... so many people from so many walks of life shared their stories and in the telling, brought history to life for me in a way that schoolbooks never did.

Why had I never heard of the intrepid women of Cumann na mBan and the Irish Citizen Army cycling around Dublin with guns and messages hidden in their baskets?

These activists and feminists thought they were fighting for a brave new world in which women and men would be equal... How bitterly disillusioned they must have felt when the new republic turned out to be dominated by men and ruled by an ultra-conservative Catholic church for decades to come.

I discovered that after the Rising came the War of Independence and the ensuing fall that was the Civil War, which created such a schism, the entire period was cloaked in silence for decades.

No wonder we didn't hear stirring accounts of how the Irish people of 1916 had mobilised themselves to take on the might of an empire and strike a blow for freedom – because those stories were intertwined with tales of families and communities at war.

I learned that whatever idealistic image the Easter Rising rebels had of an independent Republic was smashed to smithereens by the hatred and bitterness that flourished during the ensuing War of Independence and Civil War. And those fragments of shattered dreams were picked up and carried on by succeeding generations, slowly, painfully and painstakingly trying to find new ways of putting the pieces back together. In many ways, it's very much a work in progress.

I began to understand why the history books of my childhood were far from child-friendly.

The fiftieth anniversary of the Rising was commemorated in 1966, just a few years before the beginning of the Troubles in the North. Perhaps in that context, schools didn't want to court controversy by harking back to what had happened between 1916 and 1923. Maybe it was like picking at a raw wound, who knows?

What I know for sure is that history lessons in the 1970s were a yawn-fest of dates and events and I whiled them away daydreaming about Donny Osmond, or who might be at the Pres disco that weekend.

I finally left school blissfully unencumbered by any knowledge of how our past had shaped our present, but this year I got an opportunity to fill that chasm of ignorance with a new understanding and appreciation of at least one part of Irish history.

I learned how Irish people were divided in their strategies towards achieving independence, or at least some sort of self-governance, in the years before the Rising. And when our own rebellion rang out in 1916, it did so in the context of a cultural, social and political revolution that was playing out right across the globe.

I learned about civilian casualties and innocent children shot in the crossfire, businesses destroyed by the gunship Helga steaming up the Liffey, the global game-changing impact of the execution of the leaders, and how other countries took inspiration from this small nation and planned their own fight for freedom.

Most of all, I learned about deeply moving human stories, which gave me an insight into the minds and hearts of people who lived through this tumultuous period.

I spoke to people who hailed the 1916 rebels as heroes, and some who denounced them as fanatics whose actions resulted in deep political divisions that marred the country for generations.

In fact, there are so many different perspectives on the Easter Rising, it's far from a black and white issue, and it's certainly not a grey area; I see it as a riot of historical colour, like the paintings of Norman Teeling, Liam O'Neill, Laura O'Doherty and other artists who have produced such inspiring collections this year.

Commemorating the Civil War will be no easy task, but for now let's just be glad of the year we've witnessed, one that brought together communities throughout the country in local ceremonies, engaged children with imaginative schools projects, and culminated in a spectacular parade in Dublin last Easter Sunday – a rousing, peaceful, dignified event that made you glad to be there and proud to be Irish.

So now, as '*My 1916*' comes to an end, what does the Easter Rising mean to me? To my knowledge, nobody in my family was active in the rebellion, but thanks to the people who shared their stories with me, I feel as much a stakeholder in the Easter Rising as any relative.

This centenary year has been inclusive, engaging and for me, a surprising voyage of discovery. It's been an education.

Acknowledgments

Thank you Liz Kearney, Features Editor of the *Irish Independent*, for giving me the opportunity to have a go at 'My 1916' and then letting me run with it for the bones of a year until the series ended. Up to then, the only date from history that had stuck in this duffer's head was 1066, the Battle of Hastings. Random. Now it's filled with stories and people and imaginings of the Easter Rising, things I'd never have known had you not taken a chance and let me loose on something new.

When I took on the commission in summer 2015, the air was already thick with anticipation about the upcoming commemorations. Relatives' groups were mobilised into an organised structure, events were planned, individuals were trawling through Witness Statements and uncovering family histories that made their eyes pop... The centenary machine was well and truly oiled and thundering forward by the time I came on board, and I didn't have to look very far to find people to interview. On the contrary, I quickly discovered the meaning of the phrase, 'Write it and they will come.'

To follow the flow of the newspaper series, I have run the stories in this book in the same order in which they were orginally published in the *Irish Independent*.

Thank you to everybody who shared their 1916 stories with me, and for showing inordinate tolerance when explaining such a lot to somebody who knew so little. You know that spark when you connect with somebody you've never met and after half an hour, it's as if you've known each other all your lives? When that happened, it was warm and lovely and often hilarious. You know who you are.

Thank you Fergus D'Arcy for sharing your immense knowledge and wealth of contacts. Ditto Stephen Dunford, NT, for your unstinting support, enthusiasm and vast connections. Thanks also to Pauric Dempsey, Michael Loftus and Patrick Bewley for providing leads to some wonderful subjects.

Thank you Jan van Embden for being my number one proofreader, copy editor and special history adviser. Thanks for making me howl with laughter when your jaw hit the floor on hearing I was about to write a history series. Thank you for making me feel like my often idiot questions were actually valid, and for not taking offence when it became apparent (i.e. eyes glazed over) that my brain had reached overload. Thanks for the tips and tweaks, encouragement and in latter months, satisfying discussions about military strategy, cultural identity, the Rising in the context of what was happening globally at the time, and other topics that I never dreamed would one day fill our conversations when we married all those years ago.

Our daughters know more about history than I do, which wouldn't be hard. Thank you Mieke for coming up with 1916 angles I'd never have thought of on my own, and thank you Corinne for the 'hidden chicken,' Portuguese wine and pistachio cupcakes.

Finally, *go raibh maith agaibh* to the ghosts of 1916. It seems the more time passes, the more clearly you come into view.

Thanks to the curiosity of this generation using modern technology and old-fashioned graft to reach out across time and space, thousands of rank-and-file rebels, civilians, children and casualties on both sides of the divide were finally freed to rise up and take their place in the official records and in people's consciousness.

I salute you all, and I hope you hang around a while, because we have more ghosts to meet in the coming years and we need all the help we can get to face each other with dignity, understanding and respect.

Also by Celine Naughton:

Sink to Slumber

A Novel

Available now on Amazon, in a choice of
Kindle e-book or print-on-demand edition

*"Crime, deceit, betrayal, nasty family, greed and lots of unashamed
selfishness... The perfect recipe for a good page turner!"*
- Rachel Watson

*"A brisk, gripping page-turner with a clever, complex weave of plot and
with an edgy gift for characterisation. It is shot throughout with punchy,
sharp descriptive flair: and engages grippingly from the get-go..."*
- Amazon customer

www.celinenaughton.com